'With this engaging defense of Nasty Women, Janet Zuckerman joins the lineage of women writers who have turned psychoanalysis against its origins in the service of inhabiting our power, in this case by knowing and affirming our aggression. As a clinician steeped in contemporary psychoanalytic work, Zuckerman brings a plethora of insight and wisdom to bear on the deep-seated psychological obstacles to self-acceptance and expression in herself and other women. This work of reflection aims to inspire and encourage transformation, a psychoanalytic intervention fitting for our time.'

Jessica Benjamin, *Ph.D., author of* The Bonds of Love:
Psychoanalysis, Feminism and the Problem of Domination,
and Beyond Doer and Done To: Recognition Theory,
Intersubjectivity and the Third

'With this and other accomplishments, Dr. Zuckerman provides us with an in vivo illustration of highly productive nastiness. In clear and jargon-free prose, her long immersion in psychoanalytic thinking helps her lay bare the personal and cultural forces that have limited women forever, while also illustrating to us the dynamics that have enabled some, though not enough, women to liberate their aggression. This effort reflects a revolution that is long overdue. We live in a world that desperately needs many, many more nasty women like Dr. Zuckerman and her cohort.'

Irwin Hirsch, *Ph.D., NYU Postdoctoral Program
in Psychotherapy & Psychoanalysis, The William Alanson White
Institute, and the Manhattan Institute for Psychoanalysis*

'Unapologetically revealing the power of untamed, fierce, and transformative feminine energy, Zuckerman reclaims the narrative of what it means to be an aggressive woman. In a social world organized by patriarchy, aggression as it informs assertion, competition, and ambition has been welcomed, even valued, in men, while women harnessing these same forces are labeled 'nasty.' Zuckerman refreshingly illustrates the merit of female aggression using clinical interviews and historical examples and reminds readers that a woman who goes after what she wants can leverage this 'nastiness' reclaiming it not as a burden but a gift—a reminder of one's resilience and tenacity. Be tough, be ambitious, speak your mind … and if that makes you nasty … so be it! Zuckerman invites women to make use of their anger, embrace their inner darkness and the full range of their emotional lives, and defy the gender norms that only serve to limit personal experience and maintain existing power structures.'

Jean Petrucelli, *Ph.D. training and supervising analyst, The William Alanson White Institute, clinical professor and clinical consultant, NYU Postdoctoral Program in Psychotherapy & Psychoanalysis, and co-editor of* Patriarchy and its Discontents

'Through fascinating interviews with six powerful women leaders, Janet Zuckerman not only elucidates models for cultivating female agency and the constructive use of aggression within patriarchal systems but, more importantly, discerns patterns, founded in the intuitive and sometimes circuitous pathways of feminine-based power, that might be the basis for ethical resistance to the patriarchy and for nongendered, post-binary forms of leadership. Zuckerman's acute perceptiveness, empathy, and depth of interrogation—she is both a psychoanalyst and a former litigator—shine through her narrative, creating a rich, textured contemporary portrait of 'nasty women' leaders that is tender, insightful, challenging, and revelatory!'

Jill Gentile, *Ph.D., psychologist/psychoanalyst, author of* Feminine Law: Freud, Free Speech, and the Voice of Desire, *and clinical professor, NYU Postdoctoral Program in Psychotherapy & Psychoanalysis*

"Nasty Women"—Reclaiming the Power of Female Aggression

This book addresses the fraught relationship between women and aggression, one troubled by age-old patriarchal forces that disparage women's ambition, assertion, and voice.

Told from a psychoanalytic perspective, the book details the sociocultural forces that infect a woman's intrapsychic dynamics and compel her to sacrifice her goals and dreams. Compelling examples are offered from current politics, the author's own struggles with aggression, and clinical work with female patients who successfully reclaimed their aggression. The book addresses the critical question of how a woman can ever succeed, through the presentation of the author's detailed and psychoanalytically informed interviews with six powerful and highly influential women. Each woman brings to life the story of her history, influences, and challenges to provide inspiration for others to reimagine their own "nastiness" as an innovative, vitalizing tool.

This book is distinguished by its unique blend of contemporary life, psychoanalytic practice, feminist theory, and gender studies, untold in any other forum or publication. It is essential reading for psychoanalysts, psychotherapists, and all those interested in working with women in a therapeutic setting and understanding their challenges with aggression.

Janet Rivkin Zuckerman, Ph.D., is a clinical psychologist, psychoanalyst, and previously practicing attorney. She is Former Director, Faculty, and Clinical Consultant at the Westchester Center for the Study of Psychoanalysis & Psychotherapy, and Clinical Consultant at the New York University Postdoctoral Program in Psychotherapy & Psychoanalysis. She conducts supervision and study groups in interpersonal/relational psychoanalysis and is in private practice in Rye, NY.

Psychoanalysis in a New Key Book Series
Donnel Stern
Series Editor

When music is played in a new key, the melody does not change, but the notes that make up the composition do: change in the context of continuity, continuity that perseveres through change. Psychoanalysis in a New Key publishes books that share the aims psychoanalysts have always had, but that approach them differently. The books in the series are not expected to advance any particular theoretical agenda, although to this date most have been written by analysts from the Interpersonal and Relational orientations.

The most important contribution of a psychoanalytic book is the communication of something that nudges the reader's grasp of clinical theory and practice in an unexpected direction. Psychoanalysis in a New Key creates a deliberate focus on innovative and unsettling clinical thinking. Because that kind of thinking is encouraged by exploration of the sometimes surprising contributions to psychoanalysis of ideas and findings from other fields, Psychoanalysis in a New Key particularly encourages interdisciplinary studies. Books in the series have married psychoanalysis with dissociation, trauma theory, sociology, and criminology. The series is open to the consideration of studies examining the relationship between psychoanalysis and any other field—for instance, biology, literary and art criticism, philosophy, systems theory, anthropology, and political theory.

But innovation also takes place within the boundaries of psychoanalysis, and Psychoanalysis in a New Key therefore also presents work that reformulates thought and practice without leaving the precincts of the field. Books in the series focus, for example, on the significance of

"Nasty Women"—Reclaiming the Power of Female Aggression

This book addresses the fraught relationship between women and aggression, one troubled by age-old patriarchal forces that disparage women's ambition, assertion, and voice.

Told from a psychoanalytic perspective, the book details the sociocultural forces that infect a woman's intrapsychic dynamics and compel her to sacrifice her goals and dreams. Compelling examples are offered from current politics, the author's own struggles with aggression, and clinical work with female patients who successfully reclaimed their aggression. The book addresses the critical question of how a woman can ever succeed, through the presentation of the author's detailed and psychoanalytically informed interviews with six powerful and highly influential women. Each woman brings to life the story of her history, influences, and challenges to provide inspiration for others to reimagine their own "nastiness" as an innovative, vitalizing tool.

This book is distinguished by its unique blend of contemporary life, psychoanalytic practice, feminist theory, and gender studies, untold in any other forum or publication. It is essential reading for psychoanalysts, psychotherapists, and all those interested in working with women in a therapeutic setting and understanding their challenges with aggression.

Janet Rivkin Zuckerman, Ph.D., is a clinical psychologist, psychoanalyst, and previously practicing attorney. She is Former Director, Faculty, and Clinical Consultant at the Westchester Center for the Study of Psychoanalysis & Psychotherapy, and Clinical Consultant at the New York University Postdoctoral Program in Psychotherapy & Psychoanalysis. She conducts supervision and study groups in interpersonal/relational psychoanalysis and is in private practice in Rye, NY.

Psychoanalysis in a New Key Book Series
Donnel Stern
Series Editor

When music is played in a new key, the melody does not change, but
the notes that make up the composition do: change in the context of
continuity, continuity that perseveres through change. Psychoanalysis
in a New Key publishes books that share the aims psychoanalysts have
always had, but that approach them differently. The books in the series
are not expected to advance any particular theoretical agenda, although
to this date most have been written by analysts from the Interpersonal
and Relational orientations.

The most important contribution of a psychoanalytic book is the communication of something that nudges the reader's grasp of clinical theory
and practice in an unexpected direction. Psychoanalysis in a New Key
creates a deliberate focus on innovative and unsettling clinical thinking.
Because that kind of thinking is encouraged by exploration of the sometimes surprising contributions to psychoanalysis of ideas and findings
from other fields, Psychoanalysis in a New Key particularly encourages
interdisciplinary studies. Books in the series have married psychoanalysis
with dissociation, trauma theory, sociology, and criminology. The series is
open to the consideration of studies examining the relationship between
psychoanalysis and any other field—for instance, biology, literary and art
criticism, philosophy, systems theory, anthropology, and political theory.

But innovation also takes place within the boundaries of psychoanalysis, and Psychoanalysis in a New Key therefore also presents work
that reformulates thought and practice without leaving the precincts of
the field. Books in the series focus, for example, on the significance of

personal values in psychoanalytic practice, on the complex interrelationship between the analyst's clinical work and personal life, on the consequences for the clinical situation when patient and analyst are from different cultures, and on the need for psychoanalysts to accept the degree to which they knowingly satisfy their own wishes during treatment hours, often to the patient's detriment.

A full list of all titles in this series is available at:

https://www.routledge.com/Psychoanalysis-in-a-New-Key-Book-Series/book-series/LEAPNKBS

"Nasty Women"—Reclaiming the Power of Female Aggression

A Psychoanalytic Perspective

Janet Rivkin Zuckerman, Ph.D.

Routledge
Taylor & Francis Group

LONDON AND NEW YORK

Designed cover image: © Getty Images

First published 2025
by Routledge
4 Park Square, Milton Park, Abingdon, Oxon OX14 4RN

and by Routledge
605 Third Avenue, New York, NY 10158

Routledge is an imprint of the Taylor & Francis Group, an informa business

British Library Cataloguing-in-Publication Data
A catalogue record for this book is available from the British Library

Library of Congress Cataloging-in-Publication Data
Names: Zuckerman, Janet Rivkin, 1952– author.
Title: "Nasty women"—reclaiming the power of female aggression :
a psychoanalytic perspective / Janet Rivkin Zuckerman.
Description: Abingdon, Oxon ; New York, NY : Routledge, 2025. |
Series: Psychoanalysis in a new key | Includes bibliographical references
and index. |
Identifiers: LCCN 2024029021 (print) | LCCN 2024029022 (ebook) |
ISBN 9781032759029 (hardback) | ISBN 9781032759043 (paperback) |
ISBN 9781003476085 (ebook)
Subjects: LCSH: Women—United States—Psychology. |
Aggressiveness—United States. | Sex role—United States.
Classification: LCC HQ1206 .Z84 2025 (print) | LCC HQ1206 (ebook) |
DDC 155.2/32—dc23/eng/20240917
LC record available at https://lccn.loc.gov/2024029021
LC ebook record available at https://lccn.loc.gov/2024029022

ISBN: 9781032759029 (hbk)
ISBN: 9781032759043 (pbk)
ISBN: 9781003476085 (ebk)

DOI: 10.4324/9781003476085

Typeset in Times New Roman
by codeMantra

To my husband Joseph,
whose unwavering support has helped me
honor and grow my nasty woman parts.

Contents

About the Author

Janet Rivkin Zuckerman, Ph.D., is a clinical psychologist, psychoanalyst, and previously practicing attorney. She is Former Director, Faculty, and Clinical Consultant at the Westchester Center for the Study of Psychoanalysis & Psychotherapy, and Clinical Consultant at the New York University Postdoctoral Program in Psychotherapy & Psychoanalysis. She conducts supervision and study groups in interpersonal/relational psychoanalysis and is in private practice in Rye, NY. She may be reached at janet-zuckerman@gmail.com.

Acknowledgments

Much like the women interviewed for this project, I entered the crucible of writing a book through the back door. Never imagining it was something I could or would do, I only gingerly approached the idea of writing psychoanalytically when a long-ago supervisor suggested that the case we reviewed together, a little adopted girl with a strange transference, would be interesting to write about. Bolstered by my supervisor's vision of me as a writer, I began producing psychoanalytic articles and proving to a nascent voice within that I had something to say. As I continued along that path, my inner voice grew more convinced that this was so, and all was fine, or so I thought. It was only when a recent effort at an article ballooned to unruly proportions that I faced the obvious. It (not me) was needling to become a book. And so, like my interviewees, now that I am here, I feel authorized to do the job. Such is the circuitous path of many women as they dare to venture out, step by step, and let themselves be seen.

I can think of two other consequential events, besides my early supervisor, that furthered my professional journey: bowing to my family's agenda and becoming a lawyer despite a passion for psychology, and landing George Stricker as my graduate school dean and advisor.

As to my few years as a litigating attorney, they had the fortunate effect of holding up an unavoidable mirror to my own conflicts with aggression. Having to be an outsized woman with a loud, aggressive voice whose mission was to beat out others proved altogether too much for one also burdened by the patriarchal script to be well-mannered and deferential. Combining that quagmire with some good psychoanalytic therapy, however, helped me land where I am today as a psychoanalyst with much to write about.

The second fortunate event occurred when my dean and advisor at Adelphi's Derner Institute of Advanced Psychological Studies, George

Stricker, gave our first-year clinical psychology class a summer assignment to create a literature review. The catch was that we should choose a subject that grabbed our attention and spoke to us personally. If we were lucky, he counseled, the review could become the foundation for the daunting doctoral dissertation. Fortunately, I followed George's advice. And so, my study of women and aggression began, steadily growing into a dissertation, a collection of journal articles, and ultimately this book. Thank you, George Stricker. Writing about what we know and care about produces sustained interest in the subject, an in-depth learning about it and ourselves, and the chance to inspire others with that knowledge. Others who were inspirational in my early training include Martin Fisher, Robert Mendelsohn, and Lorelle Saretsky.

In my current professional life, I am first and foremost appreciative to Donnel Stern. His steady support, kindness, and recognizing voice as colleague, friend, and leader of my Thursday psychoanalytic study group, have been integral to fostering this project and encouraging me to believe it was possible. I am honored that this book is part of his series with Routledge, *Psychoanalysis in a New Key*.

A very special thanks to my colleague Jean Petrucelli, whose energy, good humor, and immense creativity are ever inspirational. Jean's fervent belief in the original version of *Nasty Women* was the indominable force that kept it alive and allowed it to swell to its current proportions. As well, Dodi Goldman was pivotal in improving my original article with his creative input and invaluable editorial suggestions. I am ever grateful to him for his contribution.

My analytic colleagues through the years have also been elemental to my growth and psychoanalytic know-how. They include those from my training and affiliation with the NYU Postdoctoral Program in Psychotherapy & Psychoanalysis—Lewis Aron, Sabe Basescu, Jessica Benjamin, Steven Botticelli, Philip Bromberg, Muriel Dimen, Jill Gentile, Adrienne Harris, Irwin Hirsch, Sheldon Itzkowitz, and Steven Mitchell—as well as others I have had the good fortune to study and grow with along the way—Jill Howard, Ruth Imber, Peter Lessem, Robert Milner, Sarah Stemp, and Donald Troise.

I have been nourished by my friends and colleagues at the Westchester Center for the Study of Psychoanalysis & Psychotherapy—Elliot Adler, Helen Adler, Diane Caspe, Ann Crane, Stewart Crane, George Goldstein, Ruth Greer, Barbara Messer, Sharon Picard, Janet Shimer, Bari Smelson,

Steven Spitz, Vera Stein, Sylvia Steinert, John Turtz, and Arnold Zinman. They have been my firm supports along with members of the long-standing study and supervision groups I lead in interpersonal and relational psycho-analysis—Sheri Gold, Diane Malkin, Christopher Nardozzi, Orly Nobel, Cheryl Rothberg, and Ramona Segreti. Together we read, study, and challenge one another in steady, meaningful conversation, ensuring that our analytic knowledge and clinical know-how remain fresh and complex.

As well, the six remarkable women I interviewed for this book have not only enabled it to happen, but also allow me to now carry them with me every day, as they continually inspire me with their courage, risk-taking, grit, and perseverance. I thank them deeply for the trust they were willing to place in a stranger who wanted to interview them about how the intimate details of their lives enabled their success. Our collaboration has been unforgettably fruitful and life-altering.

I thank my dear friend and wise colleague Isabel Kaplan for her intelligent reading and feedback on an earlier version of this manuscript and the ever-supportive publishers at Taylor & Francis, Kate Hawes, Aakriti Aggarwal, Ann King, and Georgina Clutterbuck. Their encouragement and enthusiasm about this project from the start were constant balms along my journey.

None of us would be anywhere if not for the steadfast support of loving friends with deep, historical knowledge of who we are. Most of mine are therapists as well. Thank you to Susan Livingston, who recommended the novel idea of therapy and referred me to my first therapist who assisted with the heavy lift of changing careers, John Livingston, Jon Levy, and Miriam Levy, who were integral to the creation of this book, Patricia Everett, Paula Wittlin, and Joanne Yurman.

At the end of it all, we depend upon our patients to provide the moving stories that inspire our thinking, theories, and writing. None would be possible if not for them. I am immensely thankful to all my patients for the privilege of sharing what is often the deepest, most private, and sacred aspects of their lives with me.

Finally, I am grateful to my family. I know my parents, Lenore and Leonard Rivkin, would be so proud that I have turned my own story into a book. I thank my mother for her depth, insight, and psychological-mindedness, and my father for his comfort and enjoyment of nastiness, his moxie, and his intelligence. Integrating the two of them is the bedrock of who I am today. My brother, legal eagle John Rivkin and dear sister-in-law, Nancy

Rivkin, are reliably there to lend an ear, share in the good fortunes, and weather the challenges. And of course, I extend deep thanks to my children, Scott and Matthew Zuckerman, and their spouses, Autumn Zuckerman and Nick Pandolfi, respectively. They regularly welcome my aggression and nastiness when delivered in serviceable ways and are willing partners through the difficult moments as we strive for a better place. It is my joy to see them regularly personify the insight and kindness that we tried hard to cultivate in our home. I wish for my two small grandchildren, Avery and Asher Zuckerman, the space to develop their own versions of optimal nastiness in their lives.

My husband, Joseph, has been the abiding force who has inspired me to trust that I have intelligent and significant things to say, especially when doubt envelops me. He stands by me when my own aggression begs for further regulation and partners with me as we struggle and grow together after taking it on. He helps me grow the nasty woman within me every day. For him, I am ever grateful.

Earlier versions of Part I of this book were previously published in *Contemporary Psychoanalysis*, and as a chapter in the book, *Patriarchy and its Discontents*, edited by Jean Petrucelli, Sarah Schoen, and Naomi Snider. They are presented in revised form here, and I thank Taylor & Francis, LLC for this permission.

Introduction

This book represents the culmination of my 40-year interest in the predicament of women and aggression. This was a hornet's nest I bumped into as a young person without realizing its significance, and one that steadily ballooned throughout my early professional life as a practicing litigator, a career change to psychology, and a 1988 doctoral dissertation. It is a widely recognized female entanglement that even today rears up in my life as a psychoanalytic author, instructor, supervisor, and senior clinician.

The book aims to educate the reader about the fraught relationship between women and their aggression, one that is complicated by patriarchal norms demanding them to silence a once vigorous voice and disparage their own ambition and power. The importance of this topic is underscored by its prominence in the political and social discourse of the moment, urgent calls to challenge a misogynistic system that subjugates women by insidiously passing itself off as natural, even God-given. Hiding in full view, our collusion with patriarchal restrictions that safeguard existing power structures must be named and actively challenged.

Told from a psychoanalytic perspective, the book is organized into two parts. Part I deconstructs the myriad sociocultural forces that combine with a woman's intrapsychic dynamics and compel her to forfeit her robust pre-adolescent voice of honest thoughts and feelings for one that is nice, passive, and humble as she short circuits her ambition, desires, and dreams. It demonstrates how, throughout history, a woman who acts aggressively risks being judged, shamed, and disliked. Worse, she endangers her most vital relationships. The reader is offered detailed examples of this toxic dynamic from several vantage points—the politics of the day, a personal vignette describing my struggle with aggression, and two psychoanalytically oriented case vignettes featuring female patients who were able to

DOI: 10.4324/9781003476085-1

transform their aggression into a vital, growth-promoting force in their lives.

Part II takes up the question of how any woman succeeds in living a life that reclaims her full-bodied aggression, given the entrenched cultural forces threatening to defeat her. It speaks to this critical question through the presentation of psychoanalytically informed interviews that I conducted with six powerful, successful, and highly influential working women, women I ironically refer to as "nasty." In so doing, I am disempowering a demeaning sexist slight and recruiting it to describe women who have succeeded in harnessing their aggression to actualize their goals.

The women I interviewed for the book represent different ethnicities, races, and backgrounds, and they have reached impressive stations in their chosen fields despite substantial patriarchal barriers. As each woman brings her story to life, sharing her influences and challenges, the reader enters the world of those who have successfully reintegrated their aggression and reached the top against myriad odds.

As later elaborated, my choice of the working world to demonstrate examples of successful women who have beaten back the patriarchy relies on only one particular definition of what it means for a woman to be successful. For, as we know, success is a complex term that more broadly involves each woman's effort to locate those ingredients that will make her life a meaningful one, whether in the working world or elsewhere—raising a family, engaging in meaningful volunteer efforts, or pursuing other activities not subsumed under the category of work. True as this is, however, I also emphasize the indispensability of women's ongoing participation in locations of power and influence. Their active presence reminds the world that women are up to the task of leading, and acknowledges that the issues women champion involve fundamental questions of justice and welfare that apply to women and men alike (S. D. O'Connor, 2007).

Relatedly, in choosing the working world to locate examples of women who have succeeded in using aggression constructively, I am not suggesting that this is the only arena where such conflicts flare up. In fact, the struggles addressed in this book emerge repeatedly in multiple corners of women's lives, including their social encounters, volunteer activities, marriages, and families. Most women are only too aware of this reality.

This book is distinguished by its psychoanalytic slant on the subject of women and aggression, as well as its presentation of six distinctive stories about women who have reached the top. These narratives present new and innovative strategies and perspectives that have inaugurated women's successes, in addition to offering inspiration to others that, with grit and determination, defeating patriarchal barriers is indeed possible.

Chapter 1 acquaints the reader with the troubled relationship between women and aggression, including the many cultural biases that burden it and the way women are thwarted as a result. It discusses the similarly complex relationship between psychoanalysis and the topic of aggression, including ongoing controversies about its origin and nature.

Chapter 2 describes my personal challenge with aggression in my prior profession as a litigating attorney, where I faced the irreconcilable demands of being both a forceful litigator and a passive, agreeable woman.

Chapter 3 details an interpersonal/relational psychoanalysis with Talia, who struggled with destructive aggression that poisoned her relationships. Her treatment helped her quiet early demons, which enabled her to mobilize her aggression with greater comfort and emotional regulation.

Chapter 4 describes an interpersonal/relational psychoanalysis with Emma, who had dissociated most all her aggression due to developmental trauma. Her psychoanalysis helped her reclaim and mobilize her aggression and create a less restrictive, more vibrant life as a result.

Chapter 5 offers a detailed discussion of the literature on female aggression, with sections that explore (1) patriarchy and its persistence, (2) contemporary political examples of the unresolvable problems female leaders face in credibly asserting themselves, (3) the cultural biases and developmental challenges that perpetuate patriarchal scripts, (4) the self-defeating strategies women employ to bypass these restrictive barriers, and (5) the power of psychoanalytic psychotherapy to help women reclaim a voice of power and strength.

Chapter 6 discusses the way many successful women have reached positions of power by creatively transforming traditional symbols of female disempowerment, such as nastiness or bitchiness, to their own advantage.

Chapter 7 discusses how some women find a way to transcend the patriarchal barriers against aggression and achieve success. To study this phenomenon, I conducted six psychoanalytically informed interviews with highly successful women of different ethnicities, races, and histories, exploring how their backgrounds and influences empowered their success. A detailed description of each interview is included in the following six chapters.

Chapter 8 introduces Charlotte, the first female U.S. attorney in her state. Charlotte reflects upon those family members, experiences, and places that helped her potentiate her aggression, enabling her to reach this pivotal position of power.

In Chapter 9, the reader meets Mia, the CEO of one of the largest private foundations in the United States, who describes how her family influences along with her Asian culture modeled a controlled and constructive form of aggression that she finds essential in managing the people and experiences she encounters as a powerful leader in the nonprofit world.

Chapter 10 introduces Tess, the first female dean of her law school. Tess shares the compelling story of her explosive, powerful father, who poisoned her relationship to aggression. Through a transformative psychoanalysis, Tess succeeded in recovering her dissociated aggression and converting it into an essential tool in her professional and personal life.

Chapter 11 presents Margot, one of the few Black female trauma surgeons in the medical world. Margot explains how her invaluable early experiences of maternal recognition and acceptance cemented the self-confidence, strength, and humility she calls upon daily in her life-and-death professional world, where self-control and regulated aggression are paramount. It also describes an enactment between Margot and me early in our interaction.

Chapter 12 presents Sandra, the first female federal officer of the judiciary in her state. Sandra describes her inspiring maternal grandmother, who modeled a fierce work ethic and sturdiness that undergird Sandra's role as a courtroom judge who must remain calm at all costs. This pivotal early influence was further solidified through Sandra's early experiences training horses, where regulating her aggression was also essential.

In Chapter 13, Shirley, the chief technology officer of a premier biomedical research institute and an Israeli immigrant, discusses how her success is grounded in her parental influences, family Holocaust background, and experiences in the Israeli military. These formative encounters enabled Shirley's comfort with aggression and her road to powerful leadership.

Chapter 14 details the literature on female leadership and the challenges women face in its pursuit. It includes a section on behavioral strategies that have helped women traverse patriarchal barriers.

Chapter 15 reviews the essential features of my six interviews and analyzes where each story parallels or diverges from the literature on female leadership. It concludes with an analysis of the common themes that existed across all six interviews.

Chapter 16 takes a closer look at two recurring themes in the interviews, navigating the patriarchy and the impact of each interviewee's early emotional environment. These themes are explored in the following three sections:

- "Navigating the Patriarchy and Cultural Implications" discusses the strategies utilized by the interviewees to bypass patriarchal barriers and the sociocultural implications of these choices.
- "Early Emotional Environment: Positive and Negative Implications" explores the possible effects of an early environment that de-emphasizes emotions.
- "Early Emotional Environment and its Impact on Emotional Regulation and Use of Aggression in the Interviewees" explores how these essential functions evolved historically for each interviewee.

The book's Conclusion weaves together Parts I and II, reflecting on the cultural and intrapsychic challenges women face in reclaiming and potentiating their aggression. It then reviews the way six female interviewees discovered specific strategies to navigate an unforgiving landscape that could have impeded them. Instead, they forged ahead to reach pinnacles of power, serving as impressive models of those who have succeeded in unsettling the patriarchal status quo and leaving an indelible impact on the world.

Part I

"Nasty Women"—Forging a New Narrative on Female Aggression

Chapter 1

The Problem of Women and Aggression

Back in the waning days of the 2016 U.S. presidential election, Democratic nominee Hillary Clinton was attacked in a tweet from the Republican Committee Chairman Reince Priebus. He depicted her as angry and defensive, uncomfortable, and devoid of a smile. Clinton met Priebus' slam undeterred, in the cool manner that was her way. "Actually," she said, at a forum on national security, "that's just what taking the office of president seriously, looks like" (Barrett, 2016, para. 1). And with similar composure, in the closing moments of the third and final 2016 presidential debate, Clinton steadily held her course in the midst of Donald Trump's sneering interruption, "*Such a nasty woman!*" Although Clinton's self-control during these charged moments was epic, it seems well worth asking whether any woman may be too composed in the face of such attacks—personal assaults that cry out for a strong, loud response to preserve one's dignity and self-respect. Clinton herself wondered about this very question—whether she had over-learned the lesson of staying calm and not retaliating—whether she should have told Trump, loudly and clearly, "Back up, you creep ... I know you love to intimidate women, but you can't intimidate me" (Clinton, 2017, p. 136). In other words, whether she should have dared to be more aggressive.

The unforgettable presidential election of 2016, colored by fury at and adoration for the first-ever female nominee, unleashed powerful, fresh evidence of the fraught relationship between women and aggression. It exposed the many cultural biases that silence women's once vigorous and sturdy voice, and commands them to "be nice," avoid aggressive self-assertion, and refrain from displays of anger. Men, on the other hand, have permission to use anger and rage to their personal, professional, and political advantage, as it reinforces the culture's expectation that they are strong and powerful.

DOI: 10.4324/9781003476085-3

The injunction against female aggression undergirds an entrenched patriarchal power structure that dates back for centuries and locks in the conditions of male dominance and female submissiveness. This, Hillary Clinton well understood. She struggled mightily to navigate this patriarchal pressure and the peril of crossing into its danger zone. After conferring early on with professionals on gender bias, she concluded what the majority of women implicitly know: across social sectors, men benefit from a positive relationship to aggression, power, success, and likeability, but women do not. In fact, the more aggressive, powerful, and successful a woman is, the less likeable she is perceived to be. And so it was with Clinton, who moved from a 69 percent approval rating as the U.S. Secretary of State who worked for a man, to a bombardment of attacks when she dared to reach higher and compete with one to become president.

This book reflects my long-standing interest in this toxic cultural force, one that exerts enormous pressure on women and girls, externally and internally, to silence their once sturdy voice and whittle away at what they hope to accomplish in their lives. As I researched decades ago in my doctoral dissertation on the fear of success in women, women still fear that their ambition, intelligence, and desire will be a liability if they also want to be liked, wanted, and loved. They will go as far as masking their own talents and abilities to avoid the threat of losing vital attachments. And women's fears are well-founded. Everywhere around them they are warned again and again to just be nice girls, to just "tone it down." In self-defeating compliance, women young and old end up reining themselves in to avoid feeling too large, too masculine, too loud, too much. In so doing, their subordination is further anchored in.

Having further explored this theme in the area of women's professional pursuits (Zuckerman, 1988) and their fears about public speaking (Zuckerman, 2014b), I now home in on the pervasive dynamic that instigates all these difficulties: women's troubled relationship to aggression. But before moving along, let me first discuss exactly what I mean when I use the word "aggression."

"Aggression" is a complex and problematic term that I have tangled with often in writing this book. It is one that is hard to pin down and typically provokes strong reactions, especially when applied to women. In fact, in both writing and presenting my ideas about women's difficulties with aggression, I typically receive notably divisive reactions that swing from head-nodding identification to strident disagreement that there exists any problem at all. The mere pairing of the words "women" and "aggression" seems to visibly unnerve people. As many have observed (e.g., Adichie, 2015; Traister, 2018), gender and its related patriarchal biases are so normalized, comforting, and baked into the fabric of our lives that they are rendered disturbingly invisible to most people and ultimately too destabilizing to acknowledge, no less change.

One of the many problems with the term "aggression" is that we use it in an overly broad way to capture many different human behaviors that often clash. From the more positive end, one typically less acknowledged, we use aggression to represent agency, self-assertion, healthy competition, ambition, positive risk-taking, growth, creativity, and vitality. But from the more negative end, we ask aggression to describe violence, rage, hate, hostility, dominance, envy, malevolence, and demandingness. In serving such disparate functions, the meaning of "aggression" becomes blurred and confusing.

Another complication surrounding aggression relates to the unresolved controversy in psychoanalysis about its origins and nature. From the beginning, there was an awareness that some force must exist to account for phenomena that range from positive engagement with the world of objects, all the way through to assertiveness, destructiveness, sadism, and violence. But is this force simply a feature of an instinct for self-preservation, as Freud (1909) proposed early on, or an element of the death instinct, as he later suggested (Freud, 1920)? Or perhaps aggression is better understood as a structure-building drive toward growth and motility, as conceptualized by Winnicott (1975), or a defensive reaction to environmental failures, frustrations, and impingements, as portrayed by Kohut (1972) and Thompson (1958)? Where we position aggression among these possibilities will affect the values and judgments we assign to the word. Although the etiology and nature of aggression is a more complex question beyond the scope of this work, it is still important to be clear about how I am thinking about aggression in this discussion.

Like Harris (1997), I am using the word *aggression* as a neutral, overarching concept that links the most alive, vital, creative, and constructive human forces with those that are the most hateful, malignant, and destructive. At the positive end, consider examples such as self-assertion, power, ambition, competition, and risk; at the negative end, think of hostility, rage, and violence. I am arguing that all these elements fall within the purview of aggression. This broader, more inclusive definition thus replaces the more common one that invokes only the negative dimensions of aggression, particularly when referring to women. That is, when we say a woman is aggressive, it is typically only the negative versions of the word we conjure up, reflecting the way cultural taboos against female aggression are internalized in the normative unconscious[1] and problematically perceived to be normal or natural.

The repositioning of aggression that I am advocating matters enormously for women as a remedy to offset their justifiable fears of being labeled "bitchy" or "nasty," should they assert themselves aggressively. It is, in fact, these very fears that frequently cause women to defensively shut down their voices and avoid the entire business of aggression altogether (Harris, 1997, 2002), sacrificing its healthy dimensions that are prerequisites to creating a fully potentiated life. And so, by untethering the word from its customary negative undertone (Saketopoulou, 2023),[2] I aim to neutralize its sting for women and thereby render it safer and more available for their optimal usage.

One last point before moving forward. With the broader definitions of aggression now established, I will hereafter refer to it in this book with a medley of interchangeable terms, including "power," "agency," "assertion," "ambition," "risk," and "competition" on the positive end, and "fury," "rage," and "anger" on the negative. To my mind, they all live under the banner of aggression.

Returning to the structure of this book, I continue now with a personal vignette where I use myself as an example of unresolved aggressive struggles in my prior career as a litigating attorney (Chapter 2). This is followed by two clinical examples: one where my female patient struggled with destructive aggression that poisoned her relationships (Chapter 3), and the other where a female patient had all but dissociated her aggression, leaving her passive and ineffectual in her world (Chapter 4). Both clinical narratives demonstrate how an interpersonal/relational psychoanalytic perspective can help female patients mobilize positive forms of aggression that transcend patriarchal silencing as well as their own intrapsychic obstacles. Thereafter, I review the literature on women's troubled relationship with aggression, including: the cultural and psychological factors that stifle it and thereby anchor existing power structures; women's self-compromising adaptations to these censures; and the ways psychoanalytic psychotherapy can help women raise awareness about this complex subject (Chapter 5).

Part I ends with a discussion of how women can transform traditional symbols of female disempowerment to their own advantage (Chapter 6).

Throughout the book, I include references to political firestorms, such as the 2016 U.S. presidential election and the 2018 Senate confirmation hearings of U.S. Supreme Court Justice Brett Kavanaugh, as examples of interpenetrating psychological and sociocultural factors that stigmatize women's aggression. Including these perspectives tempers the problematic tendency of psychoanalysis to separate the individual from the social, the intrapsychic from the political, and the private from the public. This predisposition relegates essential registers like the sociopolitical to the disavowed, where they become seemingly irrelevant (Rozmarin, 2017) and unavailable to address today's urgent political climate—one that begs for a psychological understanding to critique the patriarchy and foster productive dialogue in place of toxic polarization (Gilligan & Snider, 2017; Kolod, 2017).

We are reminded of this imperative as well in the history of interpersonal psychoanalysis, which emphasized the necessity of incorporating culture and environment to fully understand human character formation (Lionells et al., 1996; Thompson, 1958). This priority is further echoed in our psychoanalytic books and journals, whose recent editions directly address the current sociopolitical situation, the dangers and sacrifices of patriarchy, the necessity for social action, and the risks of isolating ourselves from disturbing current events (Gilligan & Snider, 2017; Layton & Redman, 2017). Collectively, these psychoanalytic thinkers underscore that the human condition is not only subjective and intersubjective but also equally social and political (Rozmarin, 2017). For now, though, I begin with the personal.

Notes

1 The normative unconscious is understood to be "the lived effects on identity formation of unequal power arrangements and dominant ideologies that split and differentially value straight from gay, rich from poor, masculine from feminine, white from black and brown" (Layton, 2020, p. xxxii).
2 Saketopoulou (2023) engages a similar effort as she seeks to delink the word "overwhelm" from its more common negative usage and understanding.

Chapter 2

Big Girls Don't Cry

A Personal Story

My father was a decorated World War II hero—a Silver Star from the president and two Purple Hearts marking proudly earned battle wounds. A self-made legal success, one of my father's biggest dilemmas was that I, his first-born, was a girl. I could tell it was a hard road for him.

Not surprisingly, I followed in the footsteps of a parent who was so accomplished and visibly revered during my early years. Frequently landing school leadership positions and starring roles in plays, I sported an unconflicted aggression that I naïvely thought was my due and would always be well within my reach. Like my father, I went on to become an attorney myself, not sure I would ever practice, but lulled by his narrative that a law degree was a great thing to have in one's back pocket, no matter what.

My three years studying the law were interesting and stimulating. I enjoyed them for the novelty of the subject matter, a body of learning vastly different from my liberal arts education and psychology major in college. Now, I was reading about human disputes in areas as diverse as contracts, real estate, and securities, though, even then, family law seemed the most interesting and relevant. I was well versed in being a good student and so far, my choice of the law felt fine.

Things began to get more complicated, however, when my mother asked me one day, "How do you intend to be home for your children at 3:00 pm if you're working all day as an attorney?" The question did not feel like a real question, nor a friendly one. This conversation took place during my third and final year of law school on the doorstep of my entrance to the working world. About the only sense I could make of such an odd inquiry at such a late date was that either she and my father had not aligned their hopes and dreams for my future, or that my mother felt envious and competitive, as she herself had not worked through these thorny issues; that is, how a woman

DOI: 10.4324/9781003476085-4

builds a life of both meaningful work and effective parenting. Looking back, I imagine both issues were at play, particularly given my father's propensity to dissuade (prevent) her from working at all. Given the freedom I had to construct a life of meaningful work and thriving family, envy seems quite understandable now, though at the time it was a heavy burden.

As my law school years wound down, I stayed distant enough from my own internal experience that I bypassed my growing ambivalence about being a lawyer and plowed ahead unreflectively to find a legal job. I imagine this was easier than facing the uncertainties that lurked beneath the surface.

My first stint as a lawyer was at my father's 30-"man" litigation firm. I knew this was a risky choice, given the complication that my father was at the helm, but I pushed aside those concerns and leveraged my privileged opportunity. There were no other female attorneys working at the firm when I arrived, even though a solid half of my law school class had been female. Many law firms had not yet caught up with the large influx of women emerging from law schools at that time. Working at my father's firm turned out to be another hard road, but this time it was hard for me. With no female colleagues in my midst and no existing structures to mentor newly branded attorneys, it was a lonely and scary time. But among the many challenges I faced at my father's law firm and at others where I thereafter worked in my short-lived legal career, late one particular Friday afternoon stands out.

I was 25 years old and newly graduated from law school when my father's managing partner entered my office carrying an oversized legal file with both hands. "This Monday," he announced with a wry smile, "you will be trying your first jury case in the Supreme Court of the County." As he handed over the bulky legal folder and turned to leave, I felt the blood drain from my face.

Unsteadied by this development, I headed over to my father's office to remind him that I had only been working as an attorney for four months and lacked any training at all in litigation. "How was I supposed to pull this off?" My father listened from his high-backed leather chair, and to this day I can hear his voice:

You will never be ready for your first trial before a jury, so you will start Monday. The one piece of advice I can give you, is that no matter what you do, do not cry in front of the judge.

Although I did not fully grasp the meaning of his words back then, I understand far better now that crying is something that strips away credibility and usually reads as childish immaturity. It is seen as a particularly female vulnerability, and, because of that, it is degraded (Campbell, 1993) and certainly ill-advised for a female litigator. Crying was not going to work with any judge, and evidently not with my father either. And so began my six-year stint as a female litigator.

Somehow, I managed to survive that first daunting experience and face a jury, but along the way some disquieting conflicts roared to the surface and could no longer be ignored. Succeeding in this profession, no less as my father's daughter, required a caricatured, masculine version of aggression accented by fierce confidence and fearlessness. Vulnerability or any suggestion of weakness promised a death trap, legally speaking. But the problem was, as a woman, I also suffered the patriarchal pressure to be a passive, agreeable, and likeable good girl—to be anything but aggressive. My younger self, who so jauntily sought out leadership and center stage for years, now felt beyond my grasp, suffused and submerged by a culture that smears such behavior in women and girls (see Chapter 5). In its place were the clashing profiles of my personal and professional worlds—feminine and nice, or competent and fierce. These profiles felt irreconcilable, with no apparent means of integrating the two.

As it turns out, my distress was well-founded. A study in *Law and Human Behavior* (Salerno et al., 2018), decades after the time I had been practicing, confirmed a still-existent gender bias in the legal field where women are penalized for showing anger in the courtroom, but men benefit from doing so. Angry male attorneys are perceived as commanding, powerful, competent, and hirable, but female attorneys are seen as shrill, hysterical, grating, and ineffective.[1] Given the prevalence of this double bind and the difficulty living within it (not to mention attendant sexual harassment, as further described below), many female attorneys decided to exit the profession. As one woman put it, "Men continue to recognize the softer voice, so you're constantly in turmoil. . . . Men pay lip service to feminism and equality, but the actual treatment you get is something law school never prepared you for" (Klemesrud, 1985, para. 25). For me, without any means to relationally process this Gordian knot, I sequestered my fear and vulnerability (Bromberg, 1998; D. B. Stern, 1997) and continued practicing law. My conflicts with aggression remained unaddressed for a very long time.

I have since learned that I was by no means alone in my dilemma. British researcher and social scientist Anne Campbell (1993) notes that, in fact, the most remarkable thing about girls' socialization of aggression is that there is none. Girls never learn the right way to express aggression; they learn only not to do it at all. This turns out to be a sacrifice of enormous consequence.

It is no wonder that I ultimately jettisoned my legal career for one in psychology, which appeared to have a more nuanced understanding of female aggression than the one-dimensional version typical of the law. As well, the rampant sexual harassment in the legal world at the time (to which I was no stranger) provided further reason to exit, an outgrowth of the many young women flooding the field, the many older men exploiting them, and the lack of existing sanctions at the time to stop them.

My resolve to take the leap and change careers was undergirded by some meaningful psychotherapy where I spoke aloud for the first time about my unhappy situation and was received by someone who understood how and why I might dare to consider a career other than the law. That chapter of therapeutic work helped me reclaim an earlier passion for psychology and reinforced the idea that my personal preferences actually mattered. It gave me the strength and resolve to leave behind the narrow world of my family and the law.

With all that said, my relationship to aggression remained unfinished business with the ongoing potential to ignite my fear and shame, as it is for most women. I was right that psychology and psychoanalysis held a far more complex view of the subject matter, but this difference alone could not resolve the depth of my predicament. Instead, my internal discord followed me into the consulting room, where the intimacy and authenticity of the psychoanalytic encounter demanded that it be faced and relationally dealt with. You will get a glimpse of this in the two clinical vignettes that follow.

Note

1 Things were far worse for women historically, when the traditional assumption was that the law was unsuited to women, and they were unsuited to it since their nature was to nurture (S. D. O'Connor, 2007). "Clarence Darrow was convinced that women could not be 'shining lights' at the bar 'because you are too kind. You can never be corporate lawyers because you are not cold-blooded'" (S. D. O'Connor, 2007, p. xiv). Sandra Day O'Connor observed that women's exclusion from networks of influence made it difficult, if not impossible, to disprove these patriarchal notions.

Chapter 3

Talia

I meet Talia together with her partner Brad a few months after they have begun living together as a couple in Talia's apartment. She is in her early forties, and Brad is her junior by about six years. Both patients are White, like me. Talia's insight and courage, along with her anxiety, are on full display as we begin couples therapy. Insight enables her to see that she and Brad have significant problems, courage fuels her determination to address them, and anxiety reflects her concern that their problems will defeat them. Talia is able to mobilize her impressive strength and determination when she feels solid and safe, but I learn early on in our work that these same qualities, as with most human attributes (Fromm, 1964), can easily flip into the negative; in this case, stubbornness and fury when she feels undermined or attacked.

Talia grew up in a home that was riddled with chaos and screaming, a toxic brew that was framed as ordinary communication. Her mother was highly anxious, depressed, and reactive, and her father was kinder but ineffective at reining in his explosive, critical wife. The oldest of three girls, Talia learned to cope with the turmoil of her home by lashing out with intense anger when she felt she had been treated unfairly or ignored. She was branded the problem child by her parents and siblings, since she screamed louder than the others and did not hesitate to hit members of her family when screaming proved ineffective. Talia violated the cultural mandate for girls to be nice, avoid anger, and eschew physicality, and she paid mightily for this breach with a cauldron of shame and self-hatred. Although her mother often used physical punishment to discipline her children, Talia alone was labeled the explosive and physical one in the family. In school, she was often suspended for physically fighting with female peers she felt had been disrespectful and exclusionary. She hid her hurt and vulnerability

DOI: 10.4324/9781003476085-5

in a dissociated part of herself (Bromberg, 1998) and resolved instead to get even with the bullies. Talia's compulsive need for revenge and justice is a prominent theme in our work from the outset. Poignantly, she remembers from her earliest years that all she ever wanted was someone to listen to and understand her point of view (Van der Kolk, 2014).

Brad is the youngest in his family of four and grew up with a family constellation resembling Talia's but more extreme. He explained that his mother became unhinged at the slightest provocation and was thus impossible to approach with even superficial issues, let alone serious problems. Brad mimicked his father's style of coping with his mother's emotionality—he distanced, ignored, and ridiculed her. The emotional abandonment and condescension by the family men amplified Brad's mother's dysregulation and left her isolated and humiliated. But an even more toxic dynamic in the family took hold whenever anyone questioned or disobeyed the family rules. The perceived traitor was publicly humiliated and thereby forced back in line. Brad recalls that, in reaction to his shyness about interacting with others at family events, his family would push him to the front of the room and force him to speak out. As the onlookers roared with laughter, no one grasped the cruel humiliation behind these demands, no less the damage to Brad's sense of safety and trust.

The sado-masochistic dynamic in Brad's family was ensconced by his father, who was physically abusive when his sons (not daughters) disobeyed. The profile of masculinity presented to Brad was a constricted, clichéd portrait marked by destructive aggression, supreme authority, and utter self-sufficiency, a "Man Box" (Bruni, 2017) that poisoned his relationship to his own vulnerability and mandated a disconnection from his internal world. Brad permanently shut down his emotions, sealed off from his family, and positioned himself as impenetrable. I easily empathize with his compulsive need to bulk up his muscles and erect an emotional wall that safeguards his vulnerability. Neither Talia nor Brad had parents who regularly supplied the recognition and safety that would have helped them develop emotional regulation and more useful forms of aggression. Instead, hitting, screaming, or losing one's mind, as with Brad's mother, were the standard options.

When we meet in the work, Talia is loud, angry, and defensive about most subjects, which makes it difficult to learn about the couple's story. She is easily aggrieved and reacts by loudly defending her point of view, attacking and interrupting Brad, repeating herself incessantly, and needing to win.

As she floods the sessions with words, Brad silently retreats and physically turns away. He calmly sneers at Talia's dysregulation, channeling his father's disparagement of his mother. Talia is furious at his judgment and disappearance, dynamics that mirror her family's emotional abandonment. Their pattern is embodied as Talia arches forward and Brad turns his whole body away in defiant erasure of her existence. His passive aggression is no less intense than Talia's direct attacks, though I am aware that hers feel harder to tolerate. "Always inclined to be the good girl, I shrink from feeling such aggression in myself and in other women" (Dimen, 2003, p. 235). An echo from lawyering days enters my clinical work.

We begin working on the idea that Talia and Brad learned patterns of relating to others that were modeled early on and took hold. Now mired in the details of running their lives together, they each feel stressed and easily default to their chase-and-dodge interaction, which we discuss. As I inquire into the details of their tensions, they are each able to notice more complexity in the other's experience than either one had previously realized. Talia is angry at her family's criticism that she is living with Brad but not married. Brad is highly anxious about their financial situation and unable to sleep. Hearing these emotional nuances in the safer therapeutic environment softens their defenses and makes way for new empathy between them, to their mutual surprise. New dialogue emerges in place of their emotional reactivity and effectively complicates their earlier destructive pattern.

Talia's harsh criticism and control of Brad continue, though, as does his reciprocal inability to acknowledge her anger and, importantly, its underlying distress. As an example, she feels frustrated and ignored when he refuses her requests to clean up around the house. He feels controlled and criticized, convinced it is pointless to even try to explain his experience. In another example, Talia feels threatened by Brad's constant texting with friends and angry that he refuses to ask for a raise at work. He feels intruded upon and chronically judged as insufficient. Their core themes are repeatedly enacted: She feels invisible, and he feels beaten down. Articulating these patterns adds dimensionality and space to their interactions.

I also share my perception that, when Talia voices her anger, she seems unaware that her word choice, tone, and body language carry her message as much as her content. As she considers these ideas, Brad formulates new words to agree with my observation, signaling his growing freedom in our interactions (D. B. Stern, 2015). He tells Talia that her words feel attacking, that everything he does seems wrong, and that he feels powerless to stop her onslaughts. I empathize with his futility, but in doing so, I am also concerned that Talia feels abandoned by me. This prompts me to tell her that I find her frustrations with Brad understandable—a husband's house-work can seem incomplete, Brad may be selling himself short at work, and his texting with friends can feel like a shut-out. Importantly, she feels that I recognize her subjectivity (Benjamin, 2017) and may have experienced similar feelings myself, affording me the space to also tell her that I believe she disempowers her message by the way she packages it. By emphasizing the value and insightfulness of her observations, surviving her aggression in the room, and containing her omnipotence (Winnicott, 1969), Talia's sense of safety in our relationship increases, allows for more vulnerability, and decreases her need for the shield of destructive aggression.

Working with Brad, I reframe Talia's frustrations in more modulated terms, and he continues to come forward to reveal more of himself. Talia is surprised at this shift, but also angry and frustrated that Brad is opening up to me as he continues to stonewall her. I acknowledge how hurtful this must be and ask Brad to reflect upon why talking in therapy feels different. He explains that he feels less threatened by my tone and less inflammatory words, and this frees him to engage rather than disappear.

Living safely together through these interactions promotes ongoing emo-tional growth and increased freedom in the therapeutic field (D. B. Stern, 2015), as my patients discover new space to acknowledge and confront past demons. Brad chokes back tears of shame as he shares a memory of being repeatedly slapped by his father after once disagreeing with him. He then shares a powerful fantasy where he tells his father he plans to ask for a raise at work and, when his father ridicules him by telling him he doesn't deserve it, Brad shouts out that his father is wrong and demands an apology for humiliating him. We acknowledge the importance of his emerging free-dom to aggressively confront his father in the fantasy instead of retreating in fear, as he always had done.

In Talia's case, she finds more courage to face the years of relational fall-out she endured from her destructive aggression, sharing her shame when she overheard girls gossiping about her angry outbursts and physical fighting at school. And, with great sadness, she confesses that she bullied her younger sister and feels terribly guilty about having contributed to her current dif-ficulties. She wants to apologize to her sister and asks for my help. Her decreased need to dissociate her vulnerable and empathic parts is powerful, making way for her increased integration and my more empathic view of her.

In addition to my support for Talia's subjectivity, our ability to survive highly charged enactments (Hirsch, 1993, 1996, 2008a; Layton, 2020; D. B. Stern, 2004) has helped Talia self-regulate and channel her aggression more positively. On one such occasion, as Brad is struggling to find the words to approach his employer about a raise, Talia begins shaming him about his ongoing inability to stand up and promote himself. Feeling protective of Brad and vulnerable to my own struggles with aggression, I immediately react by filling in Brad's script for him to rescue him from humiliation—I tell him what he should say to his employer. Talia feels my judgment and abandonment and begins shouting at me that I have no right to do Brad's work for him. She is right, though dysregulated by her sadistic remarks I cannot yet see it. Instead of acknowledging her insight, I deepen the enactment by loudly raising my voice to scold Talia for her meanness and insensitivity.

We all immediately realize that now I am the one who has lost my composure as I go at it head-to-head with Talia. The session draws to an abysmal close, and I immediately feel shame about my destructive aggression. Nice girls know better. When we next meet, I acknowledge that my attempted rescue of Brad was unproductive, as was my abandonment and outburst with Talia. She visibly calms with my admission, and her well of self-hatred subsides. Brad relaxes, and so do I. The power of destructive aggression to paralyze is brought under sway and detoxified through the introduction of new dialogue and the experience of repair that is unfortunately foreign to most girls and women (Dimen, 2003).

Our therapeutic enactment revealed my own destructive aggression, my shame over it, and, ultimately, my willingness to take responsibility for its hurtfulness. And, as Atlas and Aron (2017) note, our enactment became a rehearsal for a new kind of relationship that aimed toward the future rather than only repeating the past. That is, in directing her aggression squarely at me, Talia dared to test my response and risk an unknown result. Could I respond with healthy rather than reactive aggression? And if I failed, could I acknowledge that I had hurt her and be vulnerable, as I had been repeatedly advocating?

Ultimately, Talia and I were both able to find a way to tolerate our shame and accept the reality of our aggression, allowing relational reattaching to become a lived possibility, trust in repair to grow, and new freedom in the field to emerge (Benjamin, 2017; Bromberg, 2011; Schore, 2011; D. B. Stern, 2009; Tronick, 1989). As Dimen (2003) wisely advises,

"I want to argue that we must bring hatred, and all the other bad-girl feelings, forward . . . be bad as well as good" (p. 239). The acceptance and ownership of our aggression, followed by our relational repair, created new space for Talia to reintegrate positive aggressive parts she undoubtedly once possessed (Gilligan, 1982), and fostered a recalibration of dysregulated affect in us both (Zuckerman, 2014b).

Our survival and navigation of similar enacted moments have allowed Talia to feel safe and integrated enough to request some individual therapy to work on a collection of issues she herself has framed: strategies to quiet her anger, exploration of her compulsion to correct injustices, and approaches to giving constructive criticism to her subordinates at work. With impressive new vulnerability, Talia continues to work on finding creative and constructive pathways to use aggression in her life, a life that has become more rewarding and manageable as a result.

Chapter 4

Emma

At the far end of the spectrum from Talia, 40-year-old Emma is a White, pleasant, and compliant good girl. Together, she and I meet in the consulting room with little potential to disagree, let alone combust. Emma's life work has been to dissociate her once-owned aggressive parts (Bromberg, 1998; Gilligan, 1982; D. B. Stern, 2014), which she fears will permanently infect her relationships. Emma has good reason for her conviction, as her mother, Roz, is stiff, cold, and hostile, demanding that her children heed her patriarchal rules and materialistic ways without question or protest.

Emma's father, Seth, chooses the path of least resistance with his reactive wife, avoiding conflict of any kind. He fails to protect Emma from Roz and rarely encourages her independent thinking or subjectivity. But, as between Seth's dissociated aggression and Roz's overt cruelty, Emma decidedly chooses the former, since her toxic home left no space to acknowledge or relationally process problems, especially anger. Like her father, she thus dissociates her aggression and unconsciously positions herself as the nice, guileless girl who never feels her own or anyone else's anger. Yet along with this choice, Emma sacrifices her ability to stand up, self-advocate, and position herself as a positive force in her world. As Harris (1997, 2002) importantly notes, given women's anxiety about their own destructiveness, many overcompensate to avoid aggression of any kind, conflating positive forms with more negative ones that pose relational threat.

The stakes have nevertheless risen for Emma in her life, prompting her unhappiness with her mother to surface. She is married with a new mother-in-law, Audrey, who she takes to easily. When Roz demands that Emma publicly demonstrate her preference for her over Audrey, Emma quietly bucks. She feels it is only fair to share family holidays and vacations, rather than show partiality to indulge Roz's insecurities. Emma also

DOI: 10.4324/9781003476085-6

knows that her trusted path of submitting to her mother, as modeled by her father, will hurt Audrey. This predicament brings her into treatment.

As we begin, Emma has a hard time voicing what she knows to be true about her mother. Although part of her is angry that Roz ignores fairness and subjectivity, she feels fearful and disloyal about owning her own point of view and is convinced she does not have the right to do so. Hovering around us is Emma's fear of her mother's assaults and freeze-outs when confronted with any signs of her daughter's difference or separation. To avoid this danger, Emma, like her father, intuits her mother's desires and gratifies them, as she identifies herself with the aggressor (Ferenczi, 1955) and ignores her own needs.

Listening supportively to Emma, I gently share my view that her mother seems unaware that people have an internal world of thoughts and feelings that deserves recognition, as seen in her refusal to acknowledge Emma's "separate meaning-making" (Saketopoulou, 2023, p. 161). Emma considers this, but it clashes with her ritualized way of relating to Roz and signals impending danger. With time and steady therapeutic support, however, she begins to make new space to integrate the part of her that is angry at her mother's demands and the personal losses she has endured because of them. Short but iconic stories emerge about how much of her life has been tarnished because of her mother's dicta—a college semester abroad that was prohibited, her college arrival where Roz insisted she grab the best bed before her roommate arrived. In the face of her mother's urgencies, Emma begins to grasp that she has been unable to reveal her needs, either to Roz or to herself.

As the work continues to unfold, I have a growing appreciation for Emma's strong sense of justice and fair play, which has been muffled to keep Roz happy. Carmella, her childhood nanny, was a beloved surrogate who modeled an alternative, humane view of the world that quietly but powerfully seeped into Emma's sense of herself. Together in therapy, we acknowledge Emma's deep love for Carmella, the importance of her moral influence, and the poignancy that it had to be marginalized to keep Roz regulated.

I identify easily with Emma's sense of right and wrong, as well as her desire to be fair to her mother-in-law. We explore the depth of her fears about asserting herself with her mother and her strong identification with her father's dissociated aggression, as I align with her growing courage to experiment with words of difference. Together, we build and fortify an emerging self-state for Emma—one with independent ideas and the courage to face Roz's onslaughts and emotionally survive.

Despite what feels like a safe and predictable path, however, our more difficult dynamics nevertheless seep into the room, sparking an enactment. Feeling steadier together, we are ready to risk introducing aggression into our relationship. As Emma describes an emerging anxiety in her 7-year-old son Spencer, I notice that she does not seem to show much empathy for him. When a thunderstorm threatens or a school shooting is overheard on the news, Spencer unravels and refuses to leave the house. Emma grows frustrated, and, with no established tools to understand and affirm his experience, she perceives Spencer as manipulative and difficult. She also feels ashamed when her parents and friends judge Spencer as spoiled and troubled. This moves Emma into action, and, at her request, I give her the name of a colleague who works with children.

Emma does not follow through with the referral, despite my introductory call to my colleague. Her family members continue to roll their eyes at Spencer, even as Emma and I discuss the need for empathy and soothing. Emma seems relatively engaged in our discussions, although I have a nagging awareness that she is somewhat distant and not completely there. Could she be quietly resenting my ideas, annoyed at what feels like a demand to approach the problem my way, just as with her mother?

Spencer's symptoms wax and wane until another trauma strikes. This time, Emma contacts the school therapist for an appointment, attends a school presentation on children's anxiety, and buys the recommended book. She arrives at her next therapy session brimming with excitement about all she has learned from the book and proceeds to "teach me" all about how to approach anxiety in children. Or, so it felt to me at the time, as our enactment around aggression and competition steadily builds.

Much of what Emma is teaching me, we had discussed before in great detail. Her dissociation of our hard work feels irritating and hurtful, and I am becoming aware of feeling unacknowledged and uncomfortably competitive. Though it would have been easier to ignore these feelings, "coast with the status quo and maintain . . . a mutually comfortable equilibrium" (Hirsch, 2008b, p. 3), I opt instead to disrupt the calm and question her, knowing that using my countertransference is the heart of our work (Hirsch, 1996). I proceed gingerly at first, since it feels embarrassing that I am asking her for "credit" and questioning her emerging autonomy.

Me: There is something that recently came up that I thought would be important to discuss. I noticed I was having some complicated feelings when you told me about your new book on children's anxiety. I wonder if you could sense that?

Emma: Yes, in fact, I recall you reminding me that we had spoken about these things.

Me: Yes, to be honest, I was a little surprised you hadn't mentioned it. That was a little frustrating for me—it hurt a little, too.

Emma perks up, and I decide to continue:

Me: But I am also aware that, as I tell you this, I might sound a bit like your mother, who gets angry and hurt when you want to do things your own way.

Emma: That is true. I am beginning to see what you mean and the parallel involved.

Me: Even though I had some hurt and competitive feelings that you didn't mention our work, I also know how important it is for you to feel free to discover things on your own and not worry about me when you do.

Emma begins to understand that, despite my feelings, I can still respect her wishes and actions rather than constrain her emerging subjectivity to satisfy my needs. Her healthy, burgeoning aggression and separation from her father's passivity can be seen in her refusal to "give me credit" for what we had worked on and her insistence on claiming things on her own terms. As Loewald (1979, p. 756) observes,

> In the process of becoming and being an adult, significant emotional ties with parents are severed. They are not simply renounced by force of circumstances . . . but they are also actively rejected, fought against, and destroyed to varying degrees. . . . In the course of what we consider healthy development, this active urge for emancipation comes to the fore.

My hurt and angry feelings reenacted the drama of Emma and her mother whenever she tried to assert herself (Hirsch, 1993, 1996, 2008a; D. B. Stern, 2004). But once my understanding of this repetition emerged in the field (D. B. Stern, 2015), my choice of dialogue rather than retaliation cast self-assertion in a useful new light. It is possible to use aggression in a safe enough way that a woman can have her own ideas and also maintain her relationships (Bromberg, 2000). Emma did not have to lose me when she went out on her own, even though I might have been angry and hurt as a result. Her willingness to rehearse a burgeoning form of aggression with me reflects the way enactment can aim toward the future (Atlas & Aron, 2017) and access what had been mutually warded off due to unconscious normative pressures in therapist and patient alike (Layton, 2020). Ultimately, the symbolization of our mutually dissociated aggression and competition (Barth, 2018; Bromberg, 2011; D. B. Stern, 2004, 2015) cleared a new path for aggressive parts of Emma to come out of the dark and become newly integrated.

With the strong support of long-term therapy, Emma continues to locate new freedom in her life as she loosens restrictive dynamics that had previously pressured her into silence and compliance. She now believes in a daughter's right to set limits with her parents, the right to share family occasions without recrimination, and the importance of supporting her children's emerging aggression and subjectivity. With more consciousness about her impulse to subjugate her needs, Emma shares her new strategy of pausing in the face of important choices to ask herself, "How do I feel about this?" This allows her to recognize what she is feeling and address what she believes is fair and just, even when it involves disagreement or anger.

At one of our recent sessions, I smiled as Emma arrived wearing a hat that had a single word stitched across the top in block letters: FREEDOM. Without prompting, she pointed to her hat and began explaining how much freer and less frightened she feels about speaking up in her life when she feels wronged or angry; and standing up for what feels just, precisely as she learned from her beloved nanny, Carmella.

As I write, I notice that my therapeutic journey with Emma, where we access our warded-off aggression, feels far less fraught than my work with Talia, where aggression is prominently in the room and has the potential to unleash our mutual shame. Emma is one of those patients who brilliantly sidesteps aggression (Harris, 1997), as we co-create "a collusive pretense to a sisterly, mutually nurturant relationship" (Dimen, 1991, p. 346) and reassure ourselves we are nice rather than nasty women. Emma and I are better positioned for mutual growth when I allow my countertransference to notify me that I have somehow stepped on her emerging autonomy, as in our enactment around children's anxiety. In contrast, Talia and I do not enjoy the privilege of being nice girls together, and our bumpy path vividly reflects the challenge of belonging to a patriarchal culture that commands women to be nice and likeable at all costs.

Chapter 5

The Problem in Context
The Literature

As we have now seen from several different vantage points, the ability to integrate and mobilize their once full-bodied aggression remains an ongoing challenge for most women today within the dominant culture. Aggression, in its positive and negative forms, remains antithetical to stereotypical notions of femininity and often to a woman's view of herself. Instead, "silence is deeply woven into the fabric of female experience" (Simmons, 2002, p. 3), leaving women ill-equipped to fully launch their lives. Women's understandable efforts to manage this unforgiving cultural landscape poison their ability (1) to take themselves seriously and believe others will, (2) to tolerate competition and failure, (3) to constructively self-protect, and (4) to effectively master information and skills (Zuckerman, 2014b). In short, women end up sacrificing many of the tools required to build a successful and meaningful life.

I will add, however, that although the bulk of this book focuses on the difficulty most women have with their aggression, not all women and girls feel compelled to eliminate anger and conflict in their relationships. Some, in fact, feel quite comfortable with direct, negative forms of aggression (Simmons, 2002). And for girls on the margins due to race or social class, avoiding aggression, including physical aggression, may not even be an option, as I discuss in greater detail below.

It may be tempting to view contemporary culture as more accepting of women's aggression, given that (1) women feel angry as often and as deeply as men, (2) women are not "born calm" (Campbell, 1993), and (3) humans are not neurologically wired to hear the male voice but silence the female one (Beard, 2017). In actuality, however, we are far from a place where women can freely own and exercise aggression, compete, and safely embody a voice of strength and assertion (Barth, 2018; Crastnopol, 2018).

DOI: 10.4324/9781003476085-7

Though women may not feel anger any differently than men, they have less access to it (Harris, 2002) and show it differently (Radke et al., 2016; Simmons, 2002).

Persistent patriarchal scripts thus continue to denigrate women who express anger outwardly, positioning them as a perversion of nature and slapping them with labels such as crazy, overly emotional, ugly, unreasonable, unpleasant to be around, or suffering from premenstrual tension (Radke et al., 2016; Traister, 2018). This contrasts with how anger and aggression are culturally valued and encouraged in men. One journalist put it well following the 2018 testimony of Christine Blasey-Ford at Brett Kavanaugh's U.S. Senate confirmation hearings: "It was like years of academic research on display in real time, in which women who express anger will be dismissed as hysterical but men who express anger are perceived as 'passionate' about the job" (Bennett, 2018, para. 21).

Female anger is thus weaponized against women in these ways (West, 2017), exiling them into silence as this misogynistic formula embeds itself in the normative unconscious and demands "correct" identities for women, while obscuring the unequal power hierarchies it bolsters and sustains. The gendered split mandated by these toxic narratives is cemented in place with the threat that ignoring them promises the loss of love and social approval (Harris, 1997; Layton, 2020; Turkel, 2000). Though some argue that aggression has its roots in the biological, the experience and expression of it are culturally learned and similarly sustained (Simmons, 2002).

Even at the highest levels of power achieved by women, including executive boardrooms and the U.S. Supreme Court, internalized gender dynamics compel women to speak less often, use fewer words, and tolerate interruption more often than their male counterparts, who are rewarded for dominating the conversation in these ways (Liptak, 2017). Women's spoken words are also often co-opted or totally ignored by others in the room. The "failed intervention" (Beard, 2017) captures the typical experience in business and professional settings where a woman asserts a point of view that is followed by silence—and the continuation of the preceding conversation—as if the woman never opened her mouth. Such entrenched gender inequities in the workplace are further detailed in Part II of this book.

Patriarchy: Then and Now

Patriarchy is a social system that elevates some men over other men, and all men over women. It forces a split between the self-gendered masculine and the relationship-gendered feminine (Gilligan & Snider, 2018) and maintains power disproportionately in the hands of men by institutionalizing norms that favor them and withholding opportunity from women. These socially compelled rules insist on the ideals of the selfless, silent woman and the autonomous, unemotional man, guaranteeing a loss of self-assertion for those below and a loss of empathy for those on top. In so doing, these normative mandates lock in the conditions of submission and dominance and mark the psyche's induction into patriarchy (Gilligan & Snider, 2017).

The widespread public outcry against the first female U.S. presidential nominee reminded America that patriarchy is alive and well today. "In case you missed the election," Gilligan cautions, "we are still living in a patriarchy, witnessing . . . the ongoing struggle between democracy and patriarchy, love and domination" (Gilligan & Snider, 2017, p. 175). And because patriarchal scripts are so normalized, comforting, and threaded through, they are taken to be natural and not open to question. Both men and women alike avoid acknowledging and addressing gender inequities, and their entrenched virulence persists (Adichie, 2015). Gilligan and Snider (2018), however, urge us to think psychoanalytically about why and how these discriminatory forces continue.

Winnicott offers an important contribution. He believes that most people are greatly troubled by the fact that every man and every woman emerged out of a woman (Winnicott, 1975). Their difficulty with this reality is not that they were once inside and then born, but rather that they were initially completely dependent upon a woman to supply the devotion needed for healthy development. Most people hate this dependency and the emotional debt implied, and, according to Winnicott, both realities must be acknowledged and transformed into maternal gratitude if maturity is to be reached. Absent such acknowledgment, people are left with a lingering fear of dependence (Winnicott, 1975) that will always include a fear of domination. This dynamic helps explain why so few female leaders exist across political spectrums and why a man at the political top is more easily accepted and admired than a woman; that is, in most cases, there is no comparable dependency on father at the beginning.

The universal fear of women and dependency helps explain not only the pervasiveness of patriarchy, but also its early roots and impressive longevity. The ancient tale of Oedipus, involving male violence and female silence, is but one example of a classic narrative that ensconces the father's voice as the symbol of morality and the law (Gilligan & Snider, 2017). In fact, throughout Western history, there has been a radical separation between women and power, according to the renowned classics scholar Mary Beard (2017), who traces the history of misogyny from the ancient world through today. As Beard argues, Western culture has had thousands of years of practice applying the mechanisms that silence and delegitimize women, and disempower them by severing them from centers of power.

Beard (2017) locates the ancient roots of patriarchy in the classical world, where the Greeks and Romans introduced starkly gendered assumptions about female silence and the authority of the male voice. She cites Homer's *Odyssey*, dating back almost 3,000 years, as the first recorded example of a man telling a woman her voice was not to be heard in public: Telemachus, son of Odysseus and Penelope, forcefully explains to his mother that speech is the business of men, and only they know how to do it; that he holds the power in the household; and that she must return upstairs to her loom and her distaff. Penelope obediently complies. As such, Beard argues that public speaking in the classical world was not only something women did not do, but it was in fact one of the exclusive skills that defined masculinity and delegitimized women.

The beheaded Medusa, a Greek mythical figure that has long been used to demonize female authority, further underscores this patriarchal trope where Medusa's bloodied head, snaky locks, and closed eyes and lips embody the triumph of male mastery over the destructiveness and illegitimacy of female power. Throughout Western culture, Medusa has been repeatedly used to symbolize the threat of strong women who needed to be conquered; for example, by Freud, who invoked her to symbolize castration anxiety, and by anti-suffragettes, who linked suffragettes to the monster herself (Johnston, 2016).

Propelling this violent image forward to contemporary times, Beard (2017) sees the use of Medusa's bloodied head to represent a conquered Hillary Clinton in the 2016 U.S. presidential election as the starkest example of the "normalisation of gendered violence" (Beard, 2017, para. 79), where images of Trump brandishing the Clinton/Medusa head received wide public acceptance and adorned T-shirts announcing, "Life's a bitch, so don't vote for one." In contrast, a beheaded Trump/Medusa generated no less than public outrage whenever it appeared:

> The political references to Medusa only underscore the pervasive misogyny that drives many attacks against Clinton and other so-called "nasty women." . . . Indeed, almost every influential female figure has been

photoshopped with snaky hair: Martha Stewart, Condoleezza Rice, Madonna, Nancy Pelosi, Oprah Winfrey, Angela Merkel.

(Johnston, 2016, para. 2)

Unsurprisingly, Beard's outspoken female voice and forceful critique of the patriarchy, no less her decision to look unadorned and age-appropriate at age 59, have earned her online media abuse in recent years. Exploiting the anonymity of the Internet, attackers have tweeted slurs such as "a batty old broad . . . a pretentious no-nothing . . . a slut" (Tozer, 2017, paras 3–4) and superimposed her face on a pornographic image. Beard's many defenders lament that, once again, "a women [sic] in the public eye has become the focus for a storm of vile abuse" (Olusoga, 2017, para. 7), as she dares to be knowledgeable and female at the same time. Beard herself also fought back, earning the affectionate labels of troll-hunter and folk hero in the process (Schneier, 2016).

But further illustrating the thorny territory of female aggression, Beard has also sometimes expressed regret about the tenor of some of her own responses, as in the case of Oxfam's aid workers, who were sexually exploiting children following the 2008 earthquake in Haiti (R. O'Connor, 2018). In the wake of severe criticism that her tweet about this situation was condoning abuse, Beard reflected, "I really should have learned by now that it is a very bad idea to try to make a nuanced contribution to a topical debate in 280 characters. But I still do it" (Beard, 2018, para. 1).

Turning to the subject of patriarchy and its relationship with psychoanalysis, many observers maintain that Freud himself perpetuated gender inequality in his theories and ideas: according to Gentile, "Freud's legacy is nevertheless patriarchy's story" (Gentile, 2022, p. 111). This can be seen in his earliest studies on hysteria in female patients, his phallocentric construction of only a male libido, and his positioning of the penis as the sex signifier desired by all subjects, regardless of their sex (Gentile, 2022). In fact, gender binaries "have been embedded in psychoanalytic theory from the first . . . [as] most analytic theory presented a view of 'femininity' as a kind of pathological inferiority" (Seligman, 2022, p. 50). Thus, from its very inception, psychoanalysis and its core ideas have adhered to and perpetuated the unequal power structure of the patriarchal rule book, installing males as superior and dominant, and females as inferior and subordinate. This is a damaging legacy that psychoanalysis must continue to acknowledge and redress.

Patriarchal templates dating back thousands of years continue to seep into our psychoanalytic theories, as well as our views about aggression, power, and whose voices are worthy of being heard. As well, entrenched gender binaries persist in our contemporary social discourse and problematically idealize hierarchy and domination over equality and collaboration. Although we live in a world that is vastly different today, our ideas about gender have not evolved very much (Adichie, 2015).

The Catch-22 for Clinton and Blasey-Ford

As previously noted, Hillary Clinton was well versed in the cultural rules that silence women. She knew, for example, that expressing anger when Trump stalked her in the 2016 presidential debate would only hand him points and penalize her. But, while she remained controlled in her emotional expression, new criticism emerged that she was inauthentic, uncompassionate, and cold.

As many sadly noted, no matter which emotional face Clinton donned, she would inevitably be seen as aggressive, unpleasant, fake, and unlikeable, since she triggered our cultural discomfort with women who act powerfully beyond the safe boundaries of marriage and family:

> It doesn't much matter what line you take as a woman, if you venture into traditional male territory, the abuse comes anyway. It is not what you say that prompts it, it's simply the fact that you are saying it.
>
> (Beard, 2017, pp. 36–37)

Others disagree, asserting that, rather than gender, the flaw resided in Clinton herself. Critics point to her reported vindictiveness toward women who had accused her husband of sexual misconduct and her purported enabling of his behavior. They argue that these actions sullied Clinton's status as a defender of women's rights and legitimate combatant against sexual harassment. But, as with so much about the 2016 presidential race, this critique resonated strongly with those who already opposed Clinton, without moving the needle among her supporters who believed it was wrong to hold her responsible for her husband's actions (Riddell, 2016).

The 2018 confirmation hearings before the Senate Judiciary Committee following Brett Kavanaugh's nomination to the U.S. Supreme Court offered another jarring example of toxic gender dynamics that presented a no-win situation for women. In sworn testimony before the Committee, Christine Blasey-Ford challenged the historic nomination by delivering a point-by-point visceral account of her past sexual assault by Kavanaugh, a perpetrator she was 100 percent sure she knew. Disturbingly deferential, calm, and sweet, Blasey-Ford displayed none of the fury she surely felt about her chilling story, knowing full well that women are penalized for displaying anger and must appear accommodating and vulnerable instead.

Men and women alike grasped the gravity of the stakes in the Kavanaugh hearings. They dreaded that the spectacle would dissolve into nothingness and the man would once again triumph, as did Clarence Thomas decades earlier in his infamous 1991 Senate confirmation hearings, when he successfully silenced Anita Hill's accusations of sexual harassment and crude behavior. And so it was with Kavanaugh; when he took his turn to speak, the worst fears of many in fact materialized. "He snarled; he pouted and wept furiously at the injustice of having his ascendance to power interrupted by accusations of sexual assault. . . . The white men's anger had been rhetorically effective" (Traister, 2018, para. 5). Kavanaugh's indignant bluster and fury rescued him, as the committee of mostly older White men immediately joined his anger, professed there was an injustice to fix, and disengaged completely from Blasey-Ford's anguished story that challenged White male power. As PBS Correspondent Alicia Menendez pointed out, had a woman employed Kavanaugh's antics, people would have undoubtedly questioned whether she was unhinged (Bennett, 2018). "What happened inside that room was an exceptionally clear distillation of who has historically been allowed to be angry on their own behalf, and who has not" (Traister, 2018, para. 7).

The stories of Clinton, Blasey-Ford, and others present us all with an urgent reminder to notice and speak out about how often female voices are thoughtlessly degraded with innumerable toxic labels, such as "strident," "feisty," "difficult," "irritable," "bossy," "brassy," "emotional," "abrasive," "whiny," "shrill," "shrewish," and "high-maintenance." These damaging descriptors subtly but powerfully remove authority from women, often unwittingly, and relegate them back into the domestic sphere. "It is still the case that when listeners hear a female voice, they do not hear a voice that connotes authority; or rather they have not learned how to hear authority or expertise in it" (Beard, 2017, p. 30).

I am reminded of the first time I flew on an airplane and a female pilot introduced herself. It took a moment to adjust, remind myself that I was safe, and, after all that, feel proud and hopeful. The call to remember that women also embody voices of competence, strength, and authority is one that applies to everyone.

Embedded Cultural Biases

"The socialization of aggression remains one of our primary gender-linked experiences. Beginning early on and continuing through the life span, female aggression is limited and inhibited in ways both subtle and obvious" (Harris, 1997, p. 322). In fact, there is a perilous divide that typically occurs in adolescence, where young girls, who previously met the world with a strong sense of agency and capacity to voice their thoughts and feelings, gradually lose hold of these critical functions (see Chapter 2, for an example). This emptying out of authority and confidence occurs as the pressure of traditional expectations and cultural biases swells, and girls are forced to squeeze themselves into the feminine role (Gilligan et al., 1990; Taylor et al., 1995). Instead of marshalling their once authentic voice, they substitute one felt to be more socially acceptable, a "perfect girl" or "nice girl" voice, to avoid social isolation and rejection (Brown & Gilligan, 1992; Gilligan et al., 1990; Pipher, 1994). These forced adaptations alienate the girl from her inner self and exact a heavy toll on her self-esteem and confidence (Pipher, 1994).

Men and women alike succumb to the cultural stereotypes that disempower women without even realizing it. There are, of course, men who also experience conflicts, inhibitions, and shame about aggression (Dimen, 2003), like my patient Brad, who inwardly suffered from his inability to recreate his father's phallic masculinity. But I, along with others (e.g., Crastnopol, 2018), argue that the many cultural forces silencing women in the service of securing existing power structures make their road to self-actualization more hazardous and complicated.

One subliminal gender bias staunchly maintained is that women are inherently more emotional than men (Chira, 2017a). Because of this stereotype, we see women's facial expressions of emotion as coming from an internal source, rather than from a particular situation. As one psychologist studying emotional perception put it, "she's a bitch, but he's having a bad day" (Barrett, 2016, para. 6). We obey these stereotypes strictly, so when Clinton "acted presidential," and showed little emotion, she was seen as a harsh, cold, and unfeminine woman (Chira, 2017b), but when Trump insulted or attacked, he was seen as angry about a bad situation, like terrorism. He was not a "nasty man." In truth, however, we know that aggression can be applied pathologically or non-pathologically by both sexes (Chodorow, 2011).

Another cultural bias relates to the way aggression is subjectively experienced. Because existing cultural norms insist on situating aggression within a masculine context of domination and conquest, men perceive aggression as a legitimate and culturally necessary means to control others in the face of frightening forces (Campbell, 1993). Absent a less hierarchical, more collaborative view of aggression, women tend to view it as a failure of self-control that breaches the patriarchal mandate to be nice. For them, it is associated with hostility, shame, and violence to their relationships (Campbell, 1993; Garfield, 2003; Kring, 2000; Wrye, 2006), which they have been socialized to believe it is their job to protect (Gilligan & Snider, 2018; Simmons, 2002; Wrye, 2006). In this highly significant gender difference, aggression for men is justified and uncomplicated (Traister, 2018), but, for women, it is a shameful personal failing that prompts dissociation even when felt to be legitimate. The risk of being viewed as unlovable or unloving is just too great for women, whose dread of loneliness and abandonment has been widely observed (Lerner, 1980; Simmons, 2002).

Some women fear that they will be met with disapproval, specifically from men, if they act aggressively,[1] an outcome that is supported by research (Chira, 2017b). Even today, it has been shown that, when women act forcefully, men are more likely to react badly:

> Even very successful men have confessed to me that they feel intimidated by powerful women, preferring mates who are more malleable and more awed by them. . . . While the aroma of male power is an aphrodisiac for women, the perfume of female power can be a turn off for men.
>
> (Dowd, 2023b, para. 13)

Accordingly, these women worry they will be marked as undesirable life companions if they speak out, ultimately forced to live a life of lonely isolation. But, as the author Adichie, (2012, p. 29) asks, "why do we teach girls to aspire to marriage, but we don't teach boys to do the same?"

Many female voters in the 2016 election shied away from framing Clinton's candidacy as historic and showing unbridled enthusiasm for her, citing their concern that such behaviors would alienate men (Traister, 2017). Among a group of female subjects interviewed about aggression (Campbell, 1993), one explained that she fell in love with her husband precisely because she knew he would not leave if she got angry. The fear of negative reactions from men is a very real concern for many women, should they step out of the traditional bounds and act forcefully.

Implicit bias against female aggression can also be found in the nature of language itself. Cultural norms are cemented in by the choice of phallocentric terms to generally describe aggression, and female aggression is subsumed under this umbrella. Powerful women are thus problematically described in masculine bodily terms such as "ballsy" or "muscular," rather than, as some sardonically note, filled with "clitoral spunk" (Nancy Todor, quoted in Wrye, 2006, p. 74). Though language may appear impartial, it actually constructs our view of gender with such phallocentric assumptions. With only the male and his body parts in mind, the language we use subtly communicates that aggression is not an acceptable playground for women.

Adding to linguistic assumptions about aggression, male depictions of aggression dominate the media, science, and the law. It is men who write the laws, lead the armies and navies, stand at the podiums, and rally the crowds (Clinton, 2017). These formative archetypes are intentionally maintained within a masculine context of domination and conquest that omits the so-called feminine features of equality and collaboration. Trump stalking Clinton during the presidential debate, for example, was normalized and even praised by many as an acceptable example of admirable strength. Additionally, when children see men in positions of power in the office, contrasted with women packing lunches and scheduling appointments from home, this implicitly installs the message that men lead and women help (Filipovic, 2017). Women are thus robbed of models and words to shape and encourage a positive relationship to aggression (Beard, 2017; Campbell, 1993). The void that remains leaves them unprepared, confused, and relegated to the sidelines.

A problem of enormous significance thus remains—girls never learn the right way to express aggression; they only learn as they grow older not to do it at all (Campbell, 1993). "Most women have not developed tools for facing anger constructively... [only to] avoid it, deflect, or flee from it under a blanket of guilt" (Lorde, 1981, para. 31). One woman among those who

Campbell interviewed about aggression explained movingly, "I don't seem to be able to do it. So, I get very frustrated and then I cry or whatever" (Campbell, 1993, p. 46). Men, too, are confused about how to recognize and respond to women's aggression, sometimes reacting to it with condemnation, ridicule, humor, or anxiety.

When aggression arises in women's relationships with other women, many "excise [it] from their intimacy and replace it with pseudointimacy" (Dimen, 1991, p. 346). In so doing, women aim to neutralize any competition, contempt, envy, and devaluation that may emerge and feel uncomfortably reminiscent of preoedipal maternal destructiveness (Dimen, 1991).

In addition to their inability to safely assert themselves, women also typically lack the ability to repair relationships when aggression poisons them: "Femininity doesn't cover that territory at all . . . [it] provides no ritual of reparation that, in acknowledging the need to repair, transforms hate into love and thus restores ambivalence" (Dimen, 2003, p. 247). Given unavailable models of positive aggression and relational repair, as well as a dearth of research and writing on female aggression (Garfield, 2003), women remain anxious and conflicted about how to effectively launch an elemental part of self, and patriarchal inequities are thereby anchored securely in place.

The consequences of women's confusion about aggression abound in social and professional spheres alike. Many worry they are too loud or are taking up too much space and will be punished for it:

My sense that my voice was too loud, my opinions too strong, my desire dangerous, [were all] . . . an accurate assessment of . . . a world that continues to divide women into the good and the bad and to hear women's honest voices as too loud.

(Gilligan & Snider, 2017, p. 188)

Relatedly, the fear of public speaking is another arena where women's fears of aggression rear up. A common phobia for many, it is especially pronounced among women (Elise, 2008; Esposito, 2000; Zuckerman, 2014b), since it triggers conflicts around assertion, ambition, and power. That is, public speaking requires a woman to boldly take up space, stand alone, compete, and bare her vulnerabilities, which can easily be experienced in a patriarchal culture as a transgressive act that conflicts with a woman's relational identity (Person, 1982; Zuckerman, 2014b). As well, many have documented women's writing anxieties, often borne out of the fear that stepping out on the written page will similarly threaten important attachments by triggering their envy and competition (Benjamin, 2005; Grundy, 1993; Slochower, 1998; Zuckerman, 2014b).

Given the complex minefield that awaits women who forcefully assert themselves, many employ a panoply of tactics to sidestep aggression and reduce the likelihood of damaging reprisals. These defensive maneuvers include (1) disguising or reducing their achievements, (2) degrading their contributions, (3) remaining in "feminine" low-status occupations, (4) gaining vicarious satisfaction from the achievement of others, (5) adopting an overly feminine appearance to soften their presentation (Zuckerman, 1988), (6) undermining themselves, (7) self-attacking, and (8) retreating from new opportunities (Chira, 2017b).

As a poignant example of the latter, I recently underwent minor surgery, and as I interacted with my young, well-respected female anesthesiologist, I mentioned that I was working on this book. She wasted no time telling me about her ongoing discomfort in her male-dominated work environment, where her voice is routinely marginalized and the women in her field are not supported. As a result, she has little desire to pursue leadership positions, given the buffeting she anticipates and the energy she would need to withstand it. Women's pattern of dumbing down their ambition and retreating from more visible and powerful opportunities is real, indeed, in a patriarchal culture. And many talented female leaders are sacrificed along the way.

Some women opt for helping rather than leadership roles to avoid such sexist landscapes, as they correspond more closely to gendered scripts (Filipovic, 2017). Both Hillary Clinton and Sheryl Sandberg[2] describe the many women they have known who needed to be convinced they were worthy of advancement, whereas men boldly and proudly stepped up to promotions with little hesitation (Clinton, 2017; Sandberg, 2013). Women may paradoxically feel they are both too much in body, ambition, desire, and passion, but also not enough in intellect, power, and agency (Baker-Pitts, 2014).

In the social sphere, Simmons (2002) locates additional fallout from society's prohibition on open conflict for girls—a hidden culture of passive but very present alternative aggressions, such as rumors, name-calling, exclusion, and back-stabbing. These underhand tactics are launched within tightly knit social circles where they are harder to identify and more intense. And today's world of advanced technology has only exacerbated this problem given "innumerable new ways to enact adolescent torture" (Bennett, 2024, para. 7). These tactics are even more subtle, disturbing, and difficult to monitor: blocking and unblocking on social media, removing someone from a close friend's group, or constantly shifting from hot to cold in text chats to intentionally create ambiguity (Bennett, 2024). Culturally banned from more physical and direct forms of power, such "mean girls" are relegated to only nonphysical, indirect, and covert forms of aggression (Dimen, 1991; Seligson, 2024).

These findings are qualified, however, since most of what is known about girls' relationships derives from studies of only White, middle-class girls (Simmons, 2002). Simmons (2002) finds that, among girls on the margins due to social or economic struggles, aggression and self-assertion are often deeply ingrained in their lives and taught at home, since the alternatives of silence and passivity can threaten danger or invisibility. Many African American parents remind their children that, unlike their middle-class White counterparts, it is "unsafe for some girls of color to put relationships first and be 'nice' to everyone" (Simmons, 2002, p. 228). Campbell (1993) reinforces the idea that dominant middle-class notions of femininity do not apply to many marginalized populations. In her studies with girl gangs, adolescent girls who had suffered or witnessed violence at home developed a comfort with physical aggression and believed it was a necessary and permissible tool to survive. And with their faith in trust, intimacy, and relationships destroyed, they no longer feared that aggression would harm what they did not have, freeing them to use violence to insure survival (Campbell, 1993).

None of this is to say, however, that girls and women of color manage to avoid the social hazards and judgments around acting aggressively. To the contrary, in their pursuit of safety and self-protection, along with the recognition that all women seek, women of color must navigate another pernicious roadblock: the cliché of the "angry Black woman" (see my interview with Margot in Chapter 11). Michelle Obama (2018) poignantly describes her hurt and frustration that, despite her resolve to be a strong Black female, she was nevertheless stereotyped as an angry Black woman who endangered her husband's campaign and lacked gratitude for the country that made her rich and famous—another expectation saddling Black American women (Traister, 2018). The justifiable fear of encountering such smears can push women of color to further inhibit their aggression, poignantly satisfying their detractors' aim of "sweeping minority women to the perimeter" (Obama, 2018, p. 265). Given that the crucible of female aggression among other races, ethnicities, and classes has often been overlooked (Simmons,

2002), it is essential to continue learning about and studying this critical dimension.

Because aggression can feel so hazardous, uncharted, and confusing for women, they often overcompensate to avoid it. "Women too rarely make clear distinctions between agency and destructiveness, excitement and damage to others, competition and a feeling of or wish to murder" (Harris, 1997, p. 285). This elision has the effect of restricting a woman's ability to compete, achieve, and experience desire (Benjamin, 2005),[3] which inhibits her chances of receiving the acknowledgment, recognition, and pleasure she longs for and is her due (Barth, 2018).

Developmental Factors

Entwined with the pernicious cultural barriers thus far described, the character, attitudes, and behaviors of a girl's parents and family will also be central variables that shape her developing relationship to aggression. Parents will typically support those ways of being in their children that conform to social norms and discourage those that violate them. And children will in turn identify and comply with those parentally approved norms and disidentify with those deemed undesirable. The intrapsychic and the external are thus inextricably bound (Chodorow, 1978, 1995; Gilligan & Snider, 2017; Reciniello, 2011; Sandberg, 2013; Zuckerman, 2019) within the internalized normative unconscious (Layton, 2020), where the "basic mores of a particular culture are written into the developing personality" (Thompson, 1958, p. 8).

The developmental factors that can negatively impact a young girl's relationship to aggression are legion, positioning her as "a poor candidate for the normative developmental process which Winnicott suggests can open a space for agency and motility" (Harris, 1997, p. 322). Gender development is one such example: a boy's typical journey encourages his development and comfort with aggression, but a girl's path typically discourages it. That is, a boy's gender role development, at least in cases of heterosexual parents, requires an emotional withdrawal from his mother and a turn toward his father. This process carries with it the seeds of independence and competition for the boy, since he must actively move away from his dependent relationship with his mother toward autonomy, though it may also promote a problematic preoccupation with denying relationships and shunning dependency (Campbell, 1993; Chodorow, 1978). In contrast, a girl's gender role development is typically soaked in attachment and identification with her mother, with no withdrawal called for by the culture. Many believe that this pattern establishes the roots of a girl's future relational world and a tendency to overemphasize similarity and love over separation (Benjamin, 1991) and aggression, since no active turning away is required, as with her male counterparts (Chodorow, 1978; Dimen, 2003; Harris, 1997).

The character and behavior of one's mother will also significantly shape a girl's relationship to aggression. Harris (1997) notes that a mother who can live comfortably with her hatred alongside her passion for her child will be better equipped to raise a girl who is confident about her desire and subjectivity. If she rejects the cultural demands for female passivity and vulnerability, affirms and encourages her daughter to separate, she communicates confidence in her daughter's abilities and tags aggression as safe, acceptable, and useful. "Experiences of recognition allow one to resist the binary gendering of capacities such as assertion and vulnerability" (Layton, 2020, p. xxix).

However, a mother who is engulfing, controlling, and punitive, incapable of celebrating her daughter's agency, competition, risk-taking, and motility, will mark aggression as hurtful and dangerous, even something that can erase and kill (see Chapter 4 with Emma and Chapter 10 with Tess). As Dinnerstein (1976) notes, while the mother is the most vital and active presence in the mother-dominated formation of the girl's self, she can also threaten to overwhelm her needs, drown out her voice, and even encourage lapses from selfhood, given her ambivalence about her child's increasing separateness. In fact, a mother with limited ability to develop her own self will be predisposed to sabotage the autonomy of others.

Negative maternal reactions such as these can trigger a girl's guilt and conflict over ambition and success, as well as the need to soothe the mother's anger or hurt. These were prominent themes in my clinical work with Emma and in my own psychic struggles with aggression (see Chapter 2). Under such suboptimal conditions, a girl takes a silent oath not to overpower her mother, remain forever close, and sacrifice her aggression to men. She thereby wards off envious maternal attack, but also risks a lifelong tie to the maternal that becomes marked as something to be shunned by daughters and sons alike (Harris, 1997).[4]

In a similar vein, a mother who is compelled to dissociate her anger to satisfy her stereotypical gender role will be poorly suited to welcome and contain her daughter's aggression and render it safe and useful (Crastnopol, 2018). She will implicitly surrender her daughter to the so-called tyranny of the nice and kind (Brown & Gilligan, 1992), where an honest voice must be sacrificed for relationships that are idealized, alienating, and subverted by the rule that one's needs are unacceptable. Such relationships deny the complex realities of human interaction and precipitate a deep and disturbing disconnection from the self (Pipher, 1994; Simmons, 2002).

A daughter's relationship to aggression will also carry the stamp of her father's attitudes toward women. As with a mother, the more he supports the healthy expression of female aggression, encouraging competition, risk-taking, and motility, and actively rejecting patriarchal norms, the more he frees these behaviors for his daughter to integrate as acceptable parts of herself (see also Chapter 14, on the centrality of paternal involvement in a girl's development). A father's healthy relationship to his own aggression will also provide important encouragement for his daughter. My patient, Emma, unfortunately lacked such a model, as her father avoided and dissociated both his wife's aggression and his aggression toward her. This left Emma unprotected and lacking the space to process and regulate her own aggression. When a child's reflective functioning remains underdeveloped or compromised by her parents' preoccupations and defenses, as with Emma, her self-regulation and management of aggression will suffer as well (Coates, 1998; Knox, 2013; Pizer, 2003; Reckling & Buirski, 1996).

In most cases, a father's energy will be channeled toward discouraging his son from female activities and teaching him, rather than his daughter, the social value of aggression. For, unfortunately, anchoring conventional gender identities for children remains an important priority for most parents (Campbell, 1993), and one that neatly safeguards patriarchal inequities and the status quo.

What is a Woman to Do?

If women feel angry as often and as intensely as men, but are continually punished for showing it, what are they then to do with their anger? Many women bypass this dilemma by acting as if they are only nice, good girls, embodying the folklore that women are calm, do not feel anger like men, and are bitchy, hysterical, or shrill if they do (Campbell, 1993).

But this imperfect solution furthers the disabling fiction that a woman has no aggressive parts and is never hurtful. As Dimen (2003) poignantly observes, this is an impossible ideal that ignores the meanness of girls and women. It divorces them from their strength and relies on their disavowal of self (Garfield, 2003). "By washing our hands of our own capacity to injure, we perpetuate the stereotype that females are non-aggressive, [becoming] accomplices in the culture's repression of assertive women and girls by making aggression pathological, private and hidden" (Simmons, 2002, p. 193).

Crying is another response to the dilemma that female aggression is off limits. It is seen as feminine and therefore culturally acceptable, and it obeys the social rule that women should not hurt others. However, crying feeds the stereotype of female weakness and fallibility (Wrye, 2006) by associating it with breaking down, falling apart, acting childishly, or being manipulative. Ultimately, another viable avenue for women to channel their anger is thus degraded.

Without other available and acceptable outlets for their anger and aggression, some women may use physicality as a last resort. However, acting out physically is an all-out violation of the feminine rule book that will always leave humiliation and shame in its wake, just as it did with my patient Talia (see Chapter 3). Campbell (1993) poignantly describes the way men sometimes find humor in and mock women's expressions of anger and physicality, which further fuels their shame and robs them of one more outlet for their feelings.

Given the lack of legitimate ways to express anger and the enforced silencing of so much self-experience, women have "cornered the market on the seething, unspoken fury that [is] always threatening to explode" (Campbell, 1993, p. 40). Obama (2018, p. 265) agrees: "When you aren't being listened to, why wouldn't you get louder? If you're written off as angry or emotional, doesn't that just cause more of the same?" Similarly, Van der Kolk (2014, p. 354) observes that often "kids' disturbing behaviors started out as frustrated attempts to communicate distress and as misguided attempts to survive." Harris (1997) takes things a step further, citing generations of unacknowledged female rage stemming from the institutionalized silencing of women's feelings. The resulting dissociated fury is transmitted through generations, dangerously unmodulated and ultimately unusable in its fantasied, omnipotent forms.

The Role of Psychoanalytic Therapists

I see it as aspirational to communicate my acceptance and encouragement of my female patients' aggressive parts, dimensions of self that were once alive and vital, but through time forced underground by patriarchal sanctions. As psychoanalysts, we communicate this acceptance in numerous ways, such as inviting in patients' full range of emotions, as well as modeling our own aggressive risk-taking by encouraging them to tackle painful experiences, despite our fears of injuring or disrupting them (Saketopoulou, 2023).

Optimally, our accepting and open therapeutic stance toward female aggression includes not only patients' constructive agentic thoughts and actions, but also, as with my patient Talia, their loud and angry challenges as well. "A productive therapeutic stance embraces female aggression, appetite, and bigness" (Baker-Pitts, 2014, p. 303). Indeed, in women's brash and rageful expressions of aggression lie the seeds of a potentially rich and vital agency that has been otherwise buried under the weight of criticism, judgment, negation, and lack of recognition (Fromm, 1964). Talia herself said as much—no one ever listened, so she spoke louder and more angrily in her desperation to be heard and her fury at being silenced. But the residue of such an escalating cycle of aggression is debilitating shame and narcissistic injury (Garfield, 2003; Person, 1982).

Instead, by encouraging our patients to openly acknowledge and discuss their full range of feelings, particularly anger, envy, competition, and resentment, we signal our tolerance and acceptance of these difficult emotional states. This affirmation, in parallel, furthers the patient's acceptance, integration, and regulation of her own toxic affects, paving the road to transform them into constructive and usable forms (Coates, 1998; Knox, 2013; Pizer, 2003; Reckling & Buirski, 1996).[5] Vital aspects of self are thus retrieved and rendered available to disrupt the noxious and false binary of either silence or explosiveness. And, since many good girl patients regularly dissociate their aggression, therapists must look for it in disguise, such as inhibitions and reaction formations that hide transferential competition, envy, and devaluation.

When aggression is actively encouraged in these ways, patients stand to become more reflective and less reactive with others and with themselves. "Once you let these painful emotions be, they let you be . . . they can be known and managed, and hence no longer dangerous to you or anyone else" (Dimen, 2003, p. 243). In this complicated journey, therapeutic enactments will inevitably arise, as they did with my patients Talia and Emma. Therapists must trust that such enactments offer the richest opportunity to access what has been previously warded off in the face of internalized normative pressures (Layton, 2020).

We as therapists are thus called upon to develop greater tolerance for difficult and uncomfortable aggressive feelings in our female patients, particularly since we sometimes slap pejorative labels or corrosive diagnoses onto those who have difficulty controlling their aggressive impulses (Garfield, 2003).[6] In so doing, we channel the culture's difficulty tolerating women's aggression and perpetuate the dissociation of its vital positive edge. Instead, "analysts must scrupulously monitor their own aversive, silencing, rejecting responses when women get heated" (Baker-Pitts, 2014, p. 303) and take the risk of robustly engaging the aggression when it emerges.

Relatedly, it is important to avoid prematurely pressuring patients to regulate their affect, a common focus in contemporary psychoanalytic work. Though well-meaning, such an approach can feel like a familiar but problematic command for female patients to self-silence and conjure up earlier scenes where aggression was forced underground. "Analysts who rush too quickly to 'self-regulation' . . . inadvertently elevate feminine etiquette, a form of regulatory control" (Baker-Pitts, 2014, p. 303). The analyst's push for her patient to self-regulate may also insidiously serve her need to be the good girl who unwittingly highjacks the patient's emerging voice.

Thus, striking the right balance between accepting our patients' intense emotions on the one hand, and encouraging them to self-regulate on the other, can be a tricky tightrope to traverse. This is particularly so when the patient's destructive aggression is aimed directly at the therapist, who may feel it crosses the line into abusiveness and understandably push to quell it. But if, alternatively, the analyst can find her way to extend empathy, curiosity, and attunement to the pain underlying the patient's rage, the recognition and implicit acceptance this communicates will, in parallel, further the patient's acceptance and integration of these highly charged emotions. Hyperarousal will thereby be diminished as once toxic feelings become less anxiety-producing (Benjamin, 2017). In other words, as Benjamin importantly underscores, "recognition and regulation are co-determining . . . and while not exactly the same, are dynamically linked" (2017, pp. 80–81). We know this to be true from our own experience; that is, when we feel understood by another, we simply calm down (J. Benjamin, personal communication, February 21, 2014). Providing such positive therapeutic mirroring in the face of therapeutic storms is also less likely to trigger the patient's shame than direct verbal confrontation of her aggression.

Welcoming more primitive forms of aggression in our patients also requires a sophisticated awareness and understanding of our own anger, rage, and hatred. "Working clinically with aggression . . . entails, above all, comfort with one's own aggression" (Harris, 1998, p. 32). To get there, one must "travel into those dangerous sectors of yourself, the places of badness and pain" (Dimen, 2003, p. 245) that have and will continue to hurt others, as we risk accepting our own hatred of ourselves and of others. And as we accompany women on this rocky and uncertain path, psychoanalysis does its part to dismantle the binary structures of the dominant culture and foster healthy resistance to the patriarchal sanctions that paralyze women (Layton, 2020).

On this fraught journey, we therapists are not immune to the cultural forces that compel women to dissociate aggression, especially when dysregulated female patients arouse our own disowned and unresolved aggressive parts (Zuckerman, 2014a). In this regard, it is important to ask whether our defaults incorporate a healthy attitude toward female aggression. Toward being intensely disliked? What about our conflicts surrounding ambition and femininity? How have these conflicts influenced our career choices, leadership, and ambition? How have they affected our intimate relationships and the parenting of sons and daughters? What unconscious manifestations of our conflicts with aggression show up in dreams and slips?

Equally vulnerable to these social proscriptions and the anxiety they generate, I too have worried about moments where I might have violated the existing social order in this project. Might my tone have sounded too aggressive, edgy, or provocative? Conversely, have I not employed a sturdy enough voice to convey the strength of my convictions to the reader? By regularly checking in with our countertransference as it relates to these issues, we are better positioned to help our patients create a complex female identity that incorporates rather than dissociates the essential and positive dimensions of aggression—ambition, self-assertion, confidence, risk-taking, and authority.

Therapists must also help male patients explore their conflicts about working with and loving powerful women. Women's aggression, in its many forms, can harmonize with men's and mitigate the cultural pressure on men to live within a constricted concept of manhood that demands harsher forms of aggression—hypersexuality, supreme authority, and utter self-sufficiency (Miller, 2023). Therapists can also help men better understand the many faces of women's anger, including the way it reflects their understandable frustrations that self-assertion and expansion have been habitually obstructed. In so doing, male patients will be better positioned to offer encouragement and recognition to the women and girls in their lives, thereby affording them vital new pathways for personal growth and self-actualization.

Notes

1 When asked to respond to the statement "often the cost of success is greater than the reward," one respondent who was part of my dissertation research on the fear of success remarked parenthetically, ("mostly dealing with the opposite sex").

2 Although Sandberg's treatise, *Lean in*, succeeded in giving many women the courage to actualize their ambitions, numerous others have come to see it as limited. They see Sandburg as a White, Harvard-educated billionaire who recommends only individually tailored solutions to women's difficulties, rather than addressing broader systemic issues that discriminate against women in the workplace, especially women of color and low income (Goldberg, 2022).

3 Although a comprehensive discussion of the relationship between aggression and desire is beyond my scope, it is nevertheless critical to be aware of the "indissoluble nature of the interaction of libido and aggression" (Kernberg, 1991, p. 45). See also Atlas (2015) and Stoller (1979).

4 Maintaining a lifelong tie to mother and home, as such, has other, subtler effects on the developing girl, including inhibiting the development of her spatial skills and sense of direction. In societies where girls and women have limited opportunities to move independently around many different environments and practice their navigation skills, they end up with a worse sense of direction and less comfort and confidence with navigation (Ro, 2024, para. 6). This finding underscores the environmental rather than the genetic underpinnings of this skill, refuting the sexist stereotype that males are naturally better with navigation than females.

5 Remembering that these feelings were once a more acceptable, accessible, and useful part of self at an earlier time of life can facilitate this process for the patient.

6 The tendency to apply misogynistic labels and diagnoses to women is seen elsewhere in the history of psychoanalysis and medicine, as in the use of the term "hysteria," now viewed as a cultural rather than a medical condition and dropped from the DSM-III in 1980. Such patterns are understood by many as a means of controlling and pathologizing in women, that which remains mysterious, threatening, and unmanageable to men (Cohut, 2020; Devereux, 2014).

Chapter 6

"Nasty" as a Badge of Honor

Following Hillary Clinton's 2016 defeat in the U.S. presidential election, many commentators noted, and numerous T-shirts announced, that the label "bitch" had ironically gone on to become not just a curse, but also a meaningful badge of honor.

> The power of "bitch" to shame is, with a perspective adjustment, also its power to shine. All that's required to reframe the word is to point out that the things bitches are often guilty of, can be both unexceptional and necessary: flexing influence, standing up for their beliefs, not acting according to feminine norms and expectations.
>
> (Zeisler, 2016, para. 10)

In a flash, the election was reconstituted as a transformative moment that jettisoned getting along in favor of speaking up in an uncensored key.

This powerful reversal of meaning echoes the observations of many women who have successfully reached high levels of power, such as Angela Merkel, Margaret Thatcher, and Nancy Pelosi. These women have had the ingenuity and tenacity to turn the very symbols that usually disempower women into resources that helped actualize their own goals. The iconic example is Thatcher's famous handbag, which she transformed from a mundane, practical female accessory, into a weapon of power that she used metaphorically to run the country. Eventually, the most stereotypically female accessory was converted into a verb, "handbagged," denoting female political power (Beard, 2017).[1] Many of the outstanding women I interviewed for Part II of this book discuss the creative ways that they, too, have reversed the meaning of disempowering female symbols, as we shall soon see.

In just this exquisite way, being a so-called "nasty woman" can be converted into a persona worth embodying, an essential goal to aspire to, even

DOI: 10.4324/9781003476085-8

a title for a book! A propulsive force now energizes women, who are running for office and occupying positions of power in record numbers and powering the #MeToo movement to significant effect. Unless new female aggressive voices are cultivated in these ways, the realities of women's lives will remain unaddressed, their creative input tragically squandered, and female aggression will remain stigmatized rather than celebrated. "It's not your job to be likeable," says author Chimamanda Ngozi Adiche, "it's your job to be yourself" (Clinton, 2017, p. 124).

In my clinical examples, my female patients have become more of themselves through meaningful and sustained psychoanalytic work. Talia's once unbridled aggression can more often be converted into a constructive voice for healthy disagreement, rather than a blistering anger that shatters relationships. And Emma's once dissociated anger is more consciously available to convey her opinions and discontents, as she casts off the false binary of either voice or relationships. Through psychoanalytic psychotherapy, each woman now navigates her life and her relationships in more robust and complex ways, with a "pre-patriarchal human voice [that] is key to psychological resilience and political resistance" (Gilligan & Snider, 2017, p. 193). Each woman has begun to openly embrace her so-called "nasty woman" and "bitch" as essential nutrients of a more fully evolved self that understands "anger is loaded with information and energy" (Lorde, 1981, para. 20). And psychoanalysis, through its own unique language and lens, has helped address the subjective and the intersubjective, as well as the social and the political, to subdue patriarchal inequities and the silencing of women.

We will now move on to Part II of the book to study the histories, dynamics, and strategies of six professional women who succeeded in harnessing their aggression and transforming it into an indispensable tool that engineered their rise to the top.

Note

1 Despite her political skill and success, Thatcher has also been widely criticized for failing to improve the lives of women by promoting mostly men to her cabinet and claiming that the battle for women's rights had been "largely won" (Freeman, 2013). Thus, women, too, can use their aggressive strivings to perpetuate rather than resist patriarchal norms.

Part II

Becoming a "Nasty Woman"—Psychoanalytic Conversations with Women at the Top

Chapter 7

How Do Some Women Make it?

Despite our so-called modern times when it is theoretically more acceptable for women to speak out with powerful voices, and more women occupy positions of political, professional, and corporate power in America than ever before, our culture persists in judging and degrading women's aggression and leadership roles which thereby locks in their ongoing subordination:

> For decades, female leaders . . . have struggled with what political scientists call the double-bind—the difficulty of proving one's strength and competence while meeting voters' expectations of warmth, or being "likeable enough," as former President Barack Obama once said of Hillary Clinton during a 2008 primary debate.
>
> (Glueck & Lerer, 2023, para. 3)

In other words, if a woman dares to be assertive, powerful, and driven, she had best be likeable as well to survive this punitive landscape. This difficult-to-reconcile ideal—strong as well as likeable, competent as well as warm—is pervasive, confronting women across a broad and diverse spectrum that includes their social and personal interactions as well as their professional worlds. It reaches all the way to the highest ranks of society, such as female presidential candidates and justices of the U.S. Supreme Court, and sharply contrasts with the state of affairs for men. Men enjoy cultural permission to freely exhibit forcefulness and rage to their personal, professional, and political advantage, as did Brett Kavanaugh in his Senate Judiciary Committee hearings (See Chapter 5). Such behavior reinforces our culture's expectation and need for men to be aggressive and powerful.

In Part I of this book, I explored in detail how the cultural taboos against female aggression leave women feeling confused, tentative, and lost about how to reclaim and mobilize their once-owned aggression and fully launch

DOI: 10.4324/9781003476085-10

themselves. Lacking meaningful guidelines and models, many end up (1) marking healthy and necessary forms of aggression as forbidden, (2) reining themselves in to avoid feeling too masculine and too loud (Gilligan & Snider, 2017), (3) disguising and degrading achievements, (4) self-attacking and retreating from new opportunities (Chira, 2017b), and (5) opting for helping rather than leadership roles to satisfy society's strict gendered scripts (Filipovic, 2017). But in so sidestepping this incendiary cultural landscape, women also poison their ability to (1) take themselves seriously and believe others will, (2) tolerate competition and failure, (3) constructively self-protect, and (4) master information and skills (Zuckerman, 2014b). In short, women sacrifice the fundamental tools needed to build a successful and meaningful life.

The misogynistic situation I describe is familiar to most of us who are willing to look. How then is it possible for any woman to circumvent these restrictive rules and ascend to important positions of influence, power, and leadership? How can a woman harness the positive elements of her aggression, personally and professionally, to actualize her hopes and dreams and unsettle baked-in normative inequities? In Part II, I will take a closer look at these questions by peering inside the world of successful professional women and asking questions such as:

- Who are these women?
- What are their characters, psychodynamics, and parental influences?
- Is there a thematic consistency to their stories?
- What amalgam of intellect, competence, and charm (and of course appearance[1]) allows these women to sail to the top in a sociocultural surround still stuck in a stubbornly narrow view of what women can and should do with their lives?

My curiosity about all these questions led me to wonder what it would be like to sit down and speak with some of these women and consider them through a psychoanalytic lens. I wanted to explore the developmental, class, and cultural influences that allowed them to reclaim their aggression, and to study how their origins fostered the emotional regulation and safe representations of aggression that enabled their success. To do so, I decided to conduct in-depth, analytically oriented interviews by phone[2] with six highly successful women who regularly work on the frontlines. I sought out women from diverse professional settings, identities, and backgrounds, knowing that such variations would impact a woman's experience of aggression and how much freedom she feels to utilize it.

To locate my interviewees, I considered my professional and personal contacts and ultimately connected with women leaders in the legal, medical, technological, and business worlds who represent different ages, races, cultures, and geographical backgrounds.

All six women I initially contacted agreed without hesitation to be interviewed for this book. They were eager to discuss the story of their careers, the influences that launched and supported them, and the complex topic of female aggression. I was delighted and energized to offer a space for singular voices to emerge on the subject of female power and ambition, voices that reflect each woman's unique character, history, and cultural surround.

As this process unfolded, even with the limitations of distance and phone, I was ultimately able to forge an intense and deeply meaningful encounter with each of these women. They extended their trust and belief in me that together we could bring their story alive to be shared with others. From a broad set of initial questions about early home life and career, each interviewee generously and vulnerably took flight with her own views about her background, values, pride, and regrets, as well as how she has come to believe her success has been possible. I am indebted to these six women for the conversations we were ultimately able to create. For, in the end, we must all depend on the other in our efforts to create meaning and connection in our lives, since it is the interpersonal field itself that defines these possibilities. "The field is only partially our own creation. It is, to an important degree, imposed on us" (D. B. Stern, 1997, p. 156).

Before I introduce these six captivating stories, I would like to pause and reflect upon my choice of the working world to portray examples of women who have bypassed patriarchal barriers and created lives of meaning and influence. This contextual choice, namely the working environment, raises two important issues to consider, (1) what we mean when we say a woman is successful, and (2) where we locate the site of women's aggressive struggles. Let us take a closer look at each.

The Meaning of Success

In my presentation of these six stories, I often describe these women as "highly successful," given their notable professional achievements. But what exactly is it that makes them successful when compared to others, and what do we mean when we use the word "success" to describe women? In actuality, "success" is a complex term; its meaning is influenced by numerous variables, not the least being the person who is using it. My working definition of success in this book is filtered through the lens of ambition and achievement, but it is important to consider the women I might be leaving out with this choice. Can a woman be successful and constructively use her aggression if she has not chosen to work outside the home? She may have chosen to focus all her time on raising children, or work part-time to accommodate family responsibilities, or volunteer her time in activities she deems personally meaningful. Does success come down to how a particular individual subjectively defines it? Or, for that matter, how a particular culture defines it? Must a woman have both work and love in her life to feel successful and gratified, in fulfillment of Freud's famous dictum? And, importantly, have I myself unconsciously succumbed to patriarchal norms that define success from a skewed male perspective by choosing to look only at ambition and working women? As we know, that is how patriarchy sustains itself—it skulks around us, we are blind to its gendered scripts, and we default to the trap that it is natural, that this is what "normal" looks like. Success, for anyone, is simply a matter of reaching positions of influence and power in one's working life. But not so fast.

Despite abundant research about how women define success, as it turns out, one size does not fit all. Each person must carve out her own personal meaning of success; that is, what she believes will make her life satisfying and meaningful (Helgerson, 2018). Many women agree that, in the end, success means having the freedom to live by one's own values and choose one's own path. In addition, perceptions and definitions of success often change over the course of a lifetime and across generations (Wichert, 2015), as work goals and personal responsibilities come center stage at different points in life and cultural trends shift. For example, decades ago, getting married was the pinnacle of success for a woman; for Generation X, it was about advancing in male-dominated, hierarchical systems; and for Millennials, it often entails achieving better work–life balance and advancing social responsibility through a collaborative egalitarian approach (Wichert, 2015).

Even within the career and working world, success means different things to different people. For some women, pay, status, and promotion are defining; for others, success relates to self-development, recognition, autonomy, and making a difference. Gino and colleagues (2015), three self-defined professionally ambitious women at Harvard Business School, found that even when women and men believe they are equally able to reach high-level leadership positions, men want power, money, and higher positions more often than women, who have broader life goals, strive less often for powerful jobs, and anticipate negative outcomes from promotions more frequently. Interestingly, Gino and colleagues (2015, para. 27) took time to emphasize that their findings were descriptive, not prescriptive:

> Based on these data, we cannot make value judgments about whether men and women's differing views of professional advancement are good or bad, rational or irrational. . . . The findings in the paper could be construed as anti-feminist, but one could also argue that they represent true feminist ideals . . . to have a long list of goals, and to try to pursue them all. We hope our findings encourage men and women to be more aware of their own goals and preferences, and respectful of others.

Helgerson (2018) reports that women find less satisfaction in competition than men and often go out of their way to describe their success as a collaborative rather than individual endeavor. This was, in fact, the case with several of my interviewees, as we shall soon see. Though such altruistic attributions may by psychologically beneficial, they also risk women underinvesting in their own success as a result (Helgerson, 2018). Women's relationally oriented definitions of success, in contrast to those highlighting power and competition, likely reflect a culture where women are expected to remain humble and attend to the needs of others first, demonstrating how external realities powerfully influence a woman's view of herself, including whether she thinks of herself as successful (Wichert, 2015). I am reminded of Sandra Day O'Connor's decision to retire from the U.S. Supreme Court to care for her ailing husband, whereas no men on the Court facing similar circumstances have thus far done so.

Importantly, some have observed that the elements women typically cite in their definition of success—favoring relationships, feeling valued, and striving for balance—are actually open to question (Drexler, 2014). These findings assert that women will report that they value family and work–life balance over work itself, even when they do not, to satisfy the cultural expectation that they are inherently nurturing and relational. In other words, this is what women think they are supposed to say, not necessarily what they truly believe (Drexler, 2014; Rhode & Kellerman, 2007).

Supporting this hypothesis, I have heard many comments from colleagues and friends alike that reveal their ambivalence about their child-care responsibilities and their actual preference for work. "Work is easy when compared to staying at home taking care of children," or "I won't leave work until I know my kids are bathed and ready for bed," or "It is my dirty little secret that I would rather be at work than home with the kids." Poignantly, many women feel that their true sentiments can only be aired as dirty little secrets, since such feelings defy the patriarchal mandate to always prefer being at home with their children. Women are the nurturers.

Although a comprehensive review of the following issue is too large for this chapter, I will briefly touch on the ways that culture, too, influences a woman's definition of success. For example, a woman's religion may have a profound influence on how she defines her roles and, in turn, her view of success. And the values of more socially conservative sectors of society will differ from those in more progressive ones, thus impacting a woman's definition of her success. Minority populations with less access to education and opportunities may have different yardsticks to measure a woman's success; for example, the first family member to attend or graduate college or obtain licensure in a field, such as architecture, that had been previously only White and male (Margolies, 2023). And finally, there will be cross-cultural differences in how success is measured, where one culture's customs and traditions may be more traditional or progressive than another's. As an example, Suryani (2004) discusses the dilemma of Balinese women, whose primary role in their traditional culture is to foster balance and family harmony over career success, but who face the challenge of managing outside influences that are more progressive, given mass tourism, technology, and globalization.

With all the ways I have thus far stretched the meaning of success for women, I will add one final layer. I also believe that, from a broader sociocultural perspective, it is essential that women continue their quest to occupy seats of power and influence. The inclusion of women "in the room where it happens" furthers many fundamental goals: it guarantees that the world will continue to view women as viable leaders despite patriarchal pushback; it promotes gender equality (Rhode & Kellerman, 2007); it offers concrete models for future female leaders; and it underscores that "The issues women have championed are not simply women's issues; they implicate fundamental questions of justice and welfare in which both sexes have a stake" (S. D. O'Connor, 2007, p. xv). As a society, we can ill afford to suffer the loss of women's vital voices in those conversations that ultimately define the rules and laws by which we all live. "In an increasingly competitive global environment, no society can afford to hobble half its talent pool" (Rhode & Kellerman, 2007, p. 17).

Aggression in Other Contexts

My choice of the working world to present women who have transcended the patriarchy also prompts us to consider where in women's lives their conflicts with aggression rear up. It bears emphasizing that the working world is merely one of many domains where this occurs. Sadly, women's difficulties in this area manifest across most dimensions of their lives.

I know this, because I consistently hear from female patients and personal contacts alike how they feel beholden to an internal voice that commands them to appear selfless, self-sacrificing, nurturing, and kind, regardless of their true experience. Aggressive self-assertion and outright anger clash with this patriarchal mandate, and disregarding it feels frightening and relationally poisonous. Some women appear to be so cowed by this quandary that they cope by dissociating their agency and assertiveness completely, showing no conflict about feeling constrained or angry about any of these proscriptions. These are the good girls described in Part I of this book, overly cautious about hurting others and anxious about taking up too much space. They lead with only those self-states that are kind, helpful, non-confrontive, and relationally safe, thereby cordoning off essential parts of who they are. We are all likely familiar with many such women.

Suffice it to say, women's troubles with aggression appear in all aspects of their lives—marriages, friendships, and offices alike. With that proviso, I can comfortably move on to the interviews at hand, understanding that my subject matter operates well beyond its borders.

I begin by presenting the stories of six captivating women (Chapters 8 to 13),[3] followed by a review of the literature on female leadership from a psychoanalytic perspective (Chapter 14), a discussion of thematic similarities across all interviews (Chapter 15), and, finally, a closer look at two recurring themes in the interviews—navigating the patriarchy and the influence of early emotional environments (Chapter 16).

As you enter these stories, it is important to keep in mind two ideas. The first is that these narratives are entirely retrospective and thus vulnerable to the influence of time on memory, as Patchett (2023, p. 168) poignantly observes:

There is no explaining this simple truth about life: You will forget much of it. The painful things you were certain you'd never be able to let go?

Now you're not entirely sure when they happened, while the thrilling parts, the heart stopping joys, splintered and scattered and became something else.

Second, the interviews differ from a therapeutic context, which would have allowed for further inquiry and elaboration and likely produced more details about the subject at hand. Surely, there are greater nuances to each woman's story and unconscious factors that are relevant and interesting. But maintaining ongoing respect for the boundaries of the interview format and avoiding undue pressure on the interviewees were essential to maximize their felt sense of safety and trust. Within these limitations, I have attempted to maximize the information that emerged in these six compelling and illuminating stories.

Notes

1 Most women agree that attractiveness continues to be associated with respect, legitimacy, and power in their relationships with others (Diller, 2014).
2 All interviews took place during the COVID-19 pandemic beginning in 2020.
3 Pseudonyms are used for the women, who were promised confidentiality and the opportunity to review my description of our interview.

Chapter 8

Charlotte

The U.S. attorneys are the top-ranking federal law enforcement officials in each of the country's 94 judicial districts, working under the attorney general of the United States. They serve as the federal government's principal litigators in criminal and civil cases and are appointed by the president with the advice and consent of the U.S. Senate.

Charlotte, a heterosexual, sixtyish, White, upper-class woman, was the first female U.S. attorney in her state for 10 years and otherwise employed in its office for over 30 years. Smart, quick, and sassy, Charlotte was the oldest of two girls who grew up in a very small town on the eastern seaboard of the United States. She was surrounded by extended family throughout her entire childhood and told me with great pride how much she has been shaped by her origins and predecessors, six of whom were male attorneys. Charlotte nonetheless dreamed as a child that she would become a nurse:

> It was the only thing I can remember wanting to do, even though I still faint at the sight of blood! I certainly did not have a vision of being a lawyer, even though I had three relatives on one side of the street and three on the other who were lawyers, and I absorbed by osmosis my father's and grandfathers' intriguing stories about the law.

Despite her presence during these stimulating legal conversations, "there was never discussion of my professional development . . . affirmative professional development was not part of my upbringing . . . they just let me develop and my decisions were supported, encouraged, and met with great happiness." Charlotte's story reflects the way cultural shaping and the normative unconscious (Layton, 2020) constrict parental expectations and achievement for young girls. One can easily imagine a family conversation

DOI: 10.4324/9781003476085-11

more directly inclusive of Charlotte had she been a boy, one that included her "affirmative professional development."

When Charlotte told me that she had been miserable during her first semester at an elite girls' college, but worked through this and ended up loving it, I could already feel her resilience and determination at work. Her no-nonsense, practical approach and unfettered confidence that she would prevail stood out early in our interview, as it did with all my interviewees.

Charlotte attributes her stability and self-confidence to her "very strong sense of place," the small town that her ancestors had founded many decades before. But she also took pains to explain up front that "emotion was not the heart of my life." When it came to expressing her feelings outwardly:

> That was something you just didn't do—you weren't going to have a temper tantrum or a hissy fit, and you weren't going to have a breakdown and sob. You were just told if something was upsetting, just don't think about it. That carried through on both sides of my family. So, the idea of there being a lot of "I love you's" exchanged wasn't the case, but I knew my family loved me because of the way they looked at me and smiled and were interested and spent time with me. Once, I heard my maternal grandfather talking about me in a very proud manner. It was so memorable because those effusive comments were not forthcoming. It was wonderful; he was proud, and I felt buoyed up by it and strengthened by it.

I was not surprised when Charlotte then described herself as a good girl who managed her feelings alone and does not remember being angry:

> I process my feelings alone, so if I'm very upset about something or angry, I will process that by myself . . . growing up, that is what I did. I was a good girl, because I was afraid of my mother. She had a sharp tongue and wasn't one to apologize for it. I didn't want to be on the receiving end of that. For the most part, I didn't disagree; and, as I say, I have no regrets, it all worked out. But I don't remember being angry, I'd be disappointed when things wouldn't go my way, but I would process through it; I don't remember screaming or yelling. But I have to keep coming back to this governing principle: it wasn't my emotions as a female that [were] the problem; *nobody* showed emotion. When my grandfather died, my father developed overnight alopecia because of

his inability to express grief. That sort of speaks volumes about how we were . . . you just didn't talk about things. . . . So, I learned to control that.

Charlotte's father was a "fabulous human being," who was non-competitive, eschewed combativeness, and always sought conciliation despite being a lawyer. After he became a judge he gave up his law license, because the practice had become too contentious. "He could just sit and contemplate things, read and research . . . always had a book, so he was never lonely. He was more the life of the mind." Charlotte's mother, on the other hand, in her late nineties at the time we spoke, had little trouble being tart and contrary:

If I say it's Monday, she would say "it's the day after Sunday." Compromise wasn't part of our relationship—it was "do what I was told" and everything you did would reflect on the family. She was difficult, not warm and fuzzy. Her mother, my grandmother, was soft and plump and smelled like powder. I adored her, the softest person in my life, who I turned to when I think of emotions.

She continued. "So, I wonder if my decision to be a litigator is more influenced by aspects of my mother's personality than by the men in my family." I appreciated that Charlotte was putting pieces of her story together in a new way as we spoke, making our interview feel alive, generative, and mutually meaningful. In contrast to her more introverted father, she described both her grandfathers and uncle as very dominant men who had been state legislators and judges. About her paternal grandfather:

There was never a person he met who didn't love him; he had that kind of personality, projecting enormous confidence. . . . Maybe they were quivering balls of insecurity inside, but to me they were giants, and I felt encased in their armor.

It began to sound as if Charlotte benefitted from effective models of self-assertion, confidence, and healthy aggression from both women and men, and on both sides of her family.

Charlotte then shared that, since our initial contact, she had reflected upon many of her female contemporaries and concluded that they were all incredibly strong women, none of whom had particularly nurturing mothers. One was a CIA agent whose "mother was incredibly challenging and had flown planes during WWII." Another colleague was a real estate developer, one of six children and "not warm and fuzzy." The list went on and on. I enjoyed that Charlotte was weaving her own theory about the kinds of circumstances and people who might produce someone capable of being an ambitious and confident woman.

When I asked if she thought her difficult mother may have been challenging for her in other ways, Charlotte said she never questioned whether her mother loved her: "This is just who we were, where we come from, our own ethos and heredity. Your emotions are something to be fought back." Her resoluteness was powerful, an apparent guiding theme in her life that did not bear challenging. Internally, though, I wondered how such a taboo on emotional expression had affected Charlotte across her life at large, navigating the challenges of a highly demanding position and decades of personal and professional relationships (I will say more about this in Chapter 16).

When I inquired about her experiences of envy and competition, particularly from women, Charlotte explained that her sister had experienced difficulty in school due to a learning disability, and she envied Charlotte's skills and talents. For Charlotte, this was "heartbreaking." When experiencing a similar dynamic from friends, she said she prefers to call it competition rather than envy, since "my friends are very strong women, and they would never allow envy because it would be perceived as weakness. But competition, totally. And it can be used positively. I did." I saw, once again, Charlotte's impressive ability to turn an obstacle, in this case envy or competition, into something she not only perceived positively but could also use as a self-motivator.

When I inquired about risk, Charlotte's pragmatism and sturdy self-confidence again emerged. She explained that risk-taking and making decisions were an integral part of her job, when even as a young attorney she was left to figure things out on her own, though she "knew from nothing."

She recounted two powerful examples of how she trusted her intuition, took a risk, and "by the Grace of God, or whoever is overlooking this universe, they didn't come back to blow up." One year out of law school, with no supervision on the job, Charlotte had to decide whether to charge a man who had kidnapped his girlfriend. After the defense attorney told her that the defendant was in a desperate place as his girlfriend had broken up with him, Charlotte took a chance, did not charge him, and "it all worked out."

She was thrilled to learn that, a year later, the man had gotten married, become a nurse, and gone on to have children and a wonderful life.

On another occasion, prior to becoming a U.S. attorney, Charlotte had to defend a young army reservist who had taken a massive military truck to dinner with a friend, consumed a beer (but was not inebriated), and, on the way back, unknowingly hit and killed a motorcyclist. As an army reservist, he was entitled to be defended by the U.S. Attorney's office when he had to face state criminal charges. "I'm breaking out in a cold sweat just telling you this. He was a lovely man who was devastated by what had happened; he never even saw the guy." Charlotte's friend, the state prosecutor, suggested putting the man before the grand jury, which the defense rarely does, since his testimony can be used against him later. But, because Charlotte never doubted the young man's veracity and believed others would feel the same, she took the risk. He was never indicted, and, 15 years later, the man contacted Charlotte to say he had gone on to have a family and that she had no less than saved his life.

It is important to note that Charlotte did not feel these stories reflected anything special about herself; rather, she was merely doing what was required by her job. I, on the other hand, was greatly moved by both stories. Charlotte told me:

> I don't look at decision making as courageous. I look at it as something that has to be done, and when you're in a position of authority, ultimately you are the one responsible for the decisions, and you have to accept that responsibility.

What I saw was raw confidence, great compassion, and impressive humility, bound together in a complex dynamic that existed similarly among all my interviewees.

Despite her keen judgement and positive relationship to risk, Charlotte insisted that it was mainly just a "collection of good luck and circumstances that I landed at the U.S. Attorney's office." During law school, she met a prominent political figure while dining with her well-connected father. During an early internship after graduation, their paths crossed again, and the politician recommended that she apply to the U.S. Attorney's office following her clerkship. After I acknowledged her privileged position, which included family relationships with those in influential places, I then pushed back. "Don't you think your appointment also had something to do with your skills and potential?" Sticking to her guns, Charlotte added, "maybe, but there were lots of people with very strong attributes. I see it as a collection of good luck and maximizing what I had to get the job and close the deal." I quipped that, if she were a man, I was not sure she would size things up in such a humble, self-effacing way. This interchange led to another prominent theme in our meeting.

Charlotte does not perceive situations through the lens of gender. As she hinted earlier, it was not that emotions were unacceptable in her family because one was male or female; rather, nobody in her family had permission to discuss emotions. For Charlotte, leaning on gender to explain her challenges feels passive and enervating:

> I'm not one to lead with the fact that I'm a woman, because I would never have wanted to have been told early on that I was a victim. As I look back, I can remember disappointments in my childhood that I would have liked to have been sort of nurtured through, but it wasn't so. And I will take that response any day over being taught to have a victim mentality. I do know how women have been treated. There have been instances in my career where things were said, but you can't look at everybody under the same definitions. There are people who have been called "honey" and consider themselves victims of sexual harassment, but this makes it too easy for all women to feel that every slight in life is because of their gender. I am frustrated with that.

When Charlotte does consider her gender, she views it as one more asset that she uses to her advantage, a badge of honor that she makes work for her:

> I started in that office as the first woman, and all the agents were men . . . a bunch of boys. My first line of defense was humor and deflecting it back on them. I found that to be very effective. When others would sometimes make some remark, "don't you look nice today," which I always loved to hear; it was hardly offensive. I would make the same remark back to them. "Don't you look nice today," and, eventually, I'd do it before they opened their mouths. "You look fabulous—that tie!" I'd just come out with those comments. *It kind of took care of things* [emphasis added].

Her humor and lightheartedness communicated that she was not threatened or destabilized by male attention and what some might see as sexist behavior. I added: "You don't seem to have gotten stuck on gender; you discovered what could be helpful about being a woman and used it, without resentment, defensiveness, or victimhood." She agreed:

> That sounds like an outstanding summary of how I look at my career. I was born with certain attributes, and being female was one of them. To the extent it was going to help me, I didn't hesitate to use it, and to the extent it might've been used against me, I didn't choose to buy into that.

But, with a nod to the necessity of also projecting her stature and authority, Charlotte added:

> There were times at work when I got angry with agents if I was under pressure trying to put a case together and an agent was giving me trouble. And I had no problem whatsoever letting it all hang out. Really, I wasn't screaming—I find that unattractive, not a strength—but my voice might go up, and I would be very clear about my expectations.

I was impressed that her relationship to her aggression ran the gamut from lighthearted humor all the way to assertive limit-setting, and that she embodied it all with little apparent inner conflict. All of this signaled that Charlotte was comfortable with power and using it when required:

> I knew where my power lay, and I used it when I had to. I always try to assess who has the power, and I don't find a lot of people in the decision-making role who approach it from that perspective. If you have it, use it; it's a tool in your toolbox.

I noted that she had strong, positive role models for asserting power in a respectful way without the need to apologize for it. Once again, she agreed:

> I saw over the years when my relatives talked about cases and discussed their personal lives, that [power] wasn't something to be shied away from, just something in circumstances you had, or didn't have, and when you had it, you used it.

Charlotte embodied a fundamental resiliency that wove itself through our conversation. Given a roadblock to overcome, she consistently found a way to see it as something positive and use it advantageously:

When things don't go as you wish, you can indulge in self-pity because you didn't get what you want, but then you have to get over it, move along. In my worldview, you can't wallow in what hasn't gone the way you wanted in life, or you will be stuck in a never-ending spiral. People live lives of quiet desperation, because they can't help themselves out of the situation that's making them miserable. I feel sorry for them.

As we wound down our discussion, I asked Charlotte what advice she might give a daughter if she had one. She was inspirational:

Make sure she has a sense of place and the knowledge to manage the tools she is given. Everything is a tool. Anger is a tool, beauty is a tool, crying is a tool, brains are a tool. Use what you have. Temper things that might be too extreme, but don't quash any of that, and let them fly.

Chapter 9

Mia

Overseeing one of the largest private, nonprofit foundations in the United States, Mia is a 40-something, heterosexual, married, Ivy-League-educated, Asian woman with two children. She strikes me as a fascinating blend of tightly controlled aggression, affability, and intense drive. Mia comes to her position as president of a multi-billion-dollar foundation dedicated to social justice, health, and human rights, with a pre-existing belief in the importance of relationships. Immediately, I can feel how skilled she is at creating them from the way she connects with me—hoping she can be helpful and complimenting me on what she knows from our mutual connection. Her way of being is elegantly suited to a position that is fundamentally about building and maintaining strong relationships.

Mia's parents emigrated to America from South Korea in the 1980s, and she was born in the Pacific Northwest region of the United States to an upper-middle-class family. She lived in an urban environment as a young child, until her family moved to a West Coast suburb where there were very few Koreans. This was an intentional choice to afford her family more privacy and anonymity, since Mia's paternal grandfather was a well-known international figure. She was only one of three Asians in her class, and her closest friends were Italian Americans, who she described as similar to Koreans. Mia took Korean language classes growing up; she is conversational and can read and write in Korean.

Interestingly, race came up little in my conversation with Mia. Although I did inquire about it several times, my questions did not prompt further elaboration of the subject, as they did with Margot (see Chapter 11). This leaves me to wonder if the lack of details about race reflected Mia's family's emphasis on cultural adaptation; or something about where she situates race psychologically; or my way of inquiring about it in our interview.

DOI: 10.4324/9781003476085-12

I remain unsure about this question. Mia returned to South Korea every summer to see extended family, relishing these trips where she "was a celebrity, practically."

Mia always felt loved by her family, but, like Charlotte, she described them as not overly emotional or demonstrative. The youngest of three, Mia emphasized that she is most like her older brother, since both had to work harder to succeed than their gifted middle brother, an academic and athletic "super-star." She liked being preceded by a high achiever, as it offset parental pressure and taught her that she had to work hard for what she earned. "He didn't have to put in any effort, because he was always the straight A person, but this became an obstacle for him." The value of having to work hard to reach one's goals was a strong theme in our conversation and echoed Mia's family dynamics:

> My father chose to take a tougher route by coming to the United States, rather than living an easier life in South Korea with his well-connected father. *This was a blessing* [emphasis added]. Had we just led that very pampered life, we never would have had perspective, resilience, and independence, which I am most grateful for as a woman. Compared to my grantees in western Africa, walking miles for fresh water—or, thinking of my mother, who had to raise us in a foreign country predominantly by herself due to my father's work—I often reflect how fortunate we are, and stop myself from "complaining" about inconveniences. Perspective is so important.

Both Mia's parents and her paternal grandfather were strong role models for her. Her father made the life-changing choice to eschew the easier road in Korea, and her mother was active in the nonprofit world. Her paternal grandfather, the famous political figure, was "the most gregarious and charming." Taken all together, they stood for the value of work ethic, drive, and risk-taking:

> You should always be uncomfortable, take risks, make mistakes, and try new things. Many women prefer a pre-determined plan—maybe because of their biological clocks—and won't move out of their comfort zone. What's preventing great female Korean doctors from being chairs of medical departments? I think it's partly stepping out of their comfort zones, their relationship to risk. That's one that I do. I've always prided

myself in being able to live with discomfort, change, and a lot of ambiguity, unlike many. I never feared making mistakes and being uncomfortable. To be a successful, high-achieving person, you must take risks.

There was a fierceness to Mia, who was otherwise wrapped in warmth, humor, confidence, and intense focus. She could be light, as when she intentionally provoked her stoical maternal grandfather, "just a puppy on the inside," and became his favorite. Or mischievous: "My middle brother was so slick and never got caught, but I was the exact opposite." Or driven, as when she was asked by the chairman of her foundation to be the interim leader of a new West African initiative and said:

If you're going to give me the job, then give the job to me. If you don't want to give it to me, then don't, but I don't think this interim thing is good for the program . . . and that's what matters most.

The chairman ended up offering her the position permanently, and Mia accepted, though she had just had her second child 18 months after the first. Mia clearly did not shy away from hard work and new challenges. I wondered if her drive reflected not only an identification with strong, successful men, but was also a vindication of her mother, "who could have had a great career in Korea but had to stop working and cater to my father, a first-born son who was treated like a prince but couldn't put in a lightbulb."

Although Mia's self-assertiveness and confidence were loud and clear with her chairman, her relationship to aggression became more complicated as our interview unfolded. On the one hand, "in Korea, opportunities were not as available to women, and so I was always challenging that in some regard. I think I always sort of had combat boots on." She was also critical of any system that punishes women who take on part-time work for half the pay. But on the other hand, she took great pains to explain:

Anger is something I have not had to deal with personally as much myself; I see it as an issue with others, because I have less of my own anger to deal with. Confrontation, I've been able to deal with always. Probably why I'm in the position that I'm in, is just being able to navigate some challenging personalities without getting angry. I don't think anger was any more taboo in my Asian culture than anywhere else; I think it was more my personality. My grandfather, a masterful negotiator, never resorted to yelling, nor did my parents. I wasn't Type A, not a killer, ambitious, or had anger. I always negotiated instead.

Relatedly, what Mia likes least about her job is "the squeaky wheels, the stress of working with some very demanding people." But she emphasized that she does not get emotional or insulted; she maintains good working relationships and focuses on what is best for the organization. Listening to Mia, I tried to reconcile how someone so accomplished and driven could describe herself as "not Type A or ambitious." Was that her humility speaking, or more likely a premium she places on getting along with others to avoid being seen as a nasty woman? Pairing women with the idea of being aggressive generally elicits intense negative reactions from women and men alike (Zuckerman, 2019, 2022).

When I inquired about the patriarchy, Mia told me she has experienced little discrimination when compared to more extreme misogynistic stories she has heard. "You know, I *did* have to endure things along the way, of course, but I feel fortunate I was able to have the strength within myself to weather it." As with Charlotte, Mia showed resilience and measured control about sexist challenges. She contrasted her own experience with that of an older female grantee who works at a pre-eminent hospital in California. She was the only woman in her medical school class, and as an attending, was shunned by a male patient who said: "Seeing a female doctor is like seeing a dog in a white coat." Contrasting his crudeness with her own experience, Mia offered, "Now that's not something I've ever had to deal with."

She then shared another story about how she deals with misogyny:

A team member once said to me, "I can't stand the way that man was behaving, being so crude to us." I said, "why are you so bothered by this man's limitations? You're only hurting yourself." She said, "but he was so rude, and I don't care about me as much as the way he was rude to you." And I said, "but I'm not bothered by it, because he's never going to be somebody in my circle of trust." She said, "but it's somebody we have to work with." I said, "you can't impose your value system on somebody and then get angry at them. I don't want a personal relationship with him, and I'm not offended that he wants to talk about business and move on. Why get affected by this? What if he is someone important for your career advancement?" She added, "I don't want to work with that person," and I said, "you're hurting yourself in the process."

Mia's clear priority was on her grantees, her team, and her career, and she was determined not to let anything, including misogyny, get in the way of its forward motion. My reaction solidified when she added:

> Men still get away with saying and being a certain way, and women still get criticized on their appearance. No one would say, "look at that man's gut." We're still in a double standard, so I say, brush your hair! We have to deal with it.

As with Charlotte, Mia's way of dealing with sexist behavior in the workplace and female objectification was to acknowledge its existence and find a way around it, so it did not impede her, particularly working around the globe amid a vast range of cultural norms. In other words, do not overreact to unnecessary distractions or obstacles, including misogyny, and maintain a steady, even focus on your goal.

Mia attributes much of her success to the support and skills of her husband, "a great human being." Like Charlotte, she did not dwell on or boast about her achievements. Though certainly proud, she stressed that a system of supportive relationships has been integral to her ascension. Relationships and loyalty to the institution defined Mia. What she likes most about her job is "building bridges, having a strong impact, and helping society. The next generation will reap the rewards of the work we're doing now, and my focus is to invest in the institution overall." Mia is someone you would want on your team to do so.

Chapter 10

Tess

Tess, a 70-something, White, heterosexual, married woman from the eastern United States, holds the distinction of being the first female dean of her prestigious law school. She had been a female partner in a major Midwestern law firm when few women were, but opted to leave the private legal sector for academia after realizing her perfectionism interfered with her ability to delegate. "My name was always on the work," she said, explaining that this conflict would ultimately make her law firm workload impossible to carry. Tess's impressive self-awareness and considerable work in psychoanalysis stood out from the beginning in our rich, illuminating interview.

About a decade after becoming a law professor, Tess rose to become the dean of her law school. All this, despite her childhood dream of becoming Miss America. "Now it seems incredible, but that was the epitome for women. The acculturation was so different for girls. From the beginning, [boys] know that they have to be something. We didn't have that, which is a loss." Tess's parents were first-generation Americans, her father a Middle Eastern surgeon and her mother an Irish homemaker who did not graduate from high school but according to Tess, did try to improve herself. "They were in league together against the narrowness of their families, but that didn't hold them together and they divorced."

She described her father as:

An enormously successful person, very curious. He kept foreign language dictionaries on the front seat of his car, and when he got to a light, he looked at everything around him and tried to give it a name from whatever language he was working on. I learned to be a curious person.

DOI: 10.4324/9781003476085-13

But Tess quickly added:

> He was emotionally damaged, but highly functional. Sometimes I thought
> he was manic depressive because of his mood swings, but mostly I think he
> was character disordered—dominant and mercurial. A friend once said,
> "he just filled every space, and unless you fought there was no space for
> anyone else." My father saw everything in relationship to himself.

She explained that, with her mother's passive aggressiveness, her parents'
styles could not have been more different:

> My father tried to push everybody around, and she just wouldn't retreat,
> but always got what she wanted by *not* doing something. The best exam-
> ple was that he wanted her to learn how to drive, so she took all the driv-
> ing lessons, the instructor came to pick her up the day of the test, and she
> said, "I'm not going. I don't want to drive."

Given her mother's isolation, emotional unavailability, and lack of ambition, Tess's principal goal by early adolescence was to be "anything but a
homemaker." Despite loving to cook, she would intentionally "make everything horrible" when she was responsible for dinner. I asked if her maternal
disidentification was further fueled by her father's unequal treatment of her
mother. "I think tremendously so. . . . She was kind of a doormat. . . . From
an early age, 7 or 8, I figured out there was tension in the relationship."
Despite his authoritarian, explosive ways, Tess felt more loved by her
affectionate father, who wanted her to be a success, held her to very high
standards, and symbolized entry into the world at large (Benjamin, 1991).
"He actually made me compete with him in activities and in academics."
But, as with so many girls, this all changed in adolescence (Gilligan, 1982;
Pipher, 1994), "when he realized I was a girl who was beginning to develop
a critical eye toward his ideas, his wardrobe, and him," and Tess refused to
continue bolstering his fragile sense of self. With the loss of Tess's interest
in and idealization of him, her father turned his attention away, leaving her
feeling further isolated and abandoned.

Having lost the only source of recognition that she had, Tess tried desperately to find alternative ways to confirm her self-worth:

> It's not that I didn't feel loved, I think I just felt more loved by people
> outside. There was a shoemaker nearby, and he was so nice to me. I hung

around there and delivered shoes and not for pay, and my father hated it. The Episcopal church had a youth group, and it was a wonderful, peaceful place that helped me feel more whole . . . a sense of connectedness . . . the priests were better fathers. There were people who made me feel special once I got out of the house and started school.

I felt moved by what Tess was saying, as we discussed the way resilient children find substitutes for what is missing at home, an internal drive toward health that propels them to overcome suboptimal circumstances.

Tess's early and consistent academic excellence, which could have further fortified her, was also tarnished by her parents. Though her success was quietly acknowledged, her parents insisted on keeping her good grades a secret so as not to upstage her more academically and emotionally challenged sisters:

Everything had to be equal, even though we all had different needs. But my sisters always knew I was successful, and they weren't. . . . My parents would bolster them, make a fuss, and I understood exactly what they were doing. It made me feel bad for my sisters, and was confusing for them. . . . It's phony, and they knew it.

Though well-meaning, Tess's parents' way of managing her talents further complicated her relationship to success and compromised her ability to feel pride in who she was and what she had accomplished:

I learned early on that if you succeed, other people will be jealous and try to undo it, so I should be quiet. . . . When I became dean and was elevated in people's eyes, it seemed a little weird, because I was still the same person. *It took me a very long time to get over the idea that you should be quiet about your success, and you should act like it isn't success* [emphasis added]. Except when it came to my sisters, then there were parties.

These were powerful early messages that a girl's self-assertion and success will be destructive to loved ones who will feel envious and hateful because of it. This toxic dynamic sharply contrasts with the benefits that accrue from parents who position healthy female strivings as relationally safe and laudable (Zuckerman, 2019).

The process of coming to believe in her inner worth was thus contaminated early on for Tess, as she struggled to integrate the positive view of herself that so many others held. "In my twenties, I was always sure I was about to step on a banana peel and embarrass myself." The most stressful part of her professional life was the constant worry that she would fail:

For most of my life . . . a lot of people thought I was more than I thought I was . . . ultimately that worked to my benefit because I started to believe it. But I was always surprised and assumed everything I did was kind of a fluke if it was good. My sense of capability came from someone else, until middle age.

Through therapeutic work with an analyst she greatly valued, Tess discovered how dependent she was on the opinions of others and began to work hard at modifying that. "At one point, the doctor said, 'I don't even realize that my eyelid has moved, and you see it, and I then watch you change the way you're presenting something.' He knew I took my cues from other people." She continued:

My first month on the couch I only talked for the last five minutes of the session, because *I didn't know how to do it when I didn't watch* [emphasis added]. Eventually . . . I internalized a more secure view of myself.

Serious therapeutic work helped Tess understand that both positive and negative aspects of her childhood shaped her. "I had a very difficult father, and my mother was very passive aggressive, but they are also how I got to be who I am." Nowhere does this seem more apropos than with Tess's relationship to anger and aggression:

My mother had a whole different way of dealing with anger than my father. She would get angry and hit us—both were hitters—but if she was really mad, she would get cold . . . totally civil, as if nothing had changed, but it was obvious something had, and you could plead with her, "I know you're mad at me." "No, I'm not mad at you." I adopted that growing up.

Things were different with Tess's father. He would explode frequently, but, after calming down, he would forgive. "It would just go away, and he'd be friendly. It was confusing." I added, "confusing, because without any discussion it was as if the argument never happened." Tess agreed, explaining that she and her father had "knock down drag outs" when she was older, but those were about social issues that felt safe, never about their relationship. In an extreme example of a parent incapable of constructively dealing with anger, Tess's father cut ties with his daughters and told them they should feel free to change their last name (his name) after they made the difficult decision to not attend his wedding to his second wife soon after his divorce. Tess and her two sisters tried for years to reconcile with him, but their father never responded. Tess reflected:

> I'm a person who had tremendous issues dealing with and feeling anger, until I met my husband. Growing up, I adopted my mother's style of aggression . . . [not] my father's explosive thing. . . . When I met my husband, he said he could feel me freeze when I was angry, but I couldn't or wouldn't express it. I didn't even know something had made me angry, I just buried it someplace, and then I was Miss Eskimo.

"Like your mom," I added. She replied:

> Yes. My father's explosive anger made me very frightened of anger. My husband sometimes yelled, too, before he began therapy. Not at somebody, but at a frustrating situation. I would start to cry, and it was truly terrifying. Once, he said, "you're angry with me," and I was totally unconscious that I was. Luckily . . . in therapy, I could figure out why I was angry at him. Another time, I yelled at him when he'd been with his ex-wife . . . completely stunned at what came out of me. But it made me realize how much I cared about him.

Through therapy and a trusted marital relationship, Tess developed a more positive view of her anger, where integrating rather than dissociating it yielded new information, in this case her intense love for and attachment to her husband. Nonetheless, the specter of anger has remained a lifelong challenge, including on the job. Tess explained that she was initially the associate dean of her law school but hated the role, as she had to deal with:

> faculty's sometimes bombastic, uncooperative ways. It's like the difference between people who want to partner and collaborate and people who say, "I know the best way to teach, and it's better than everyone

else's." I tend to avoid conflict in my work life and found it stressful to deal with colleagues who thrive on it.

Tess's constant turmoil in her role as associate dean drove her back into therapy: "I probably couldn't have gotten through it myself. He gave me tools. When you are dean, it's different. There's this institution, you're leading it and moving forward is what's important. It was easier to keep the anger at bay."

Tess eventually learned to think of her aggression as a tool rather than a monster to avoid. As with Charlotte and Mia, she relied on humor to regulate hostility that arose around her:

I got very adept at using nice humor to tweak somebody without being sarcastic. I was able to diffuse a lot of situations that could have made me angry. With the guys, I'd been their colleague long before I was dean, so there was the usual guy behavior, but it wasn't too bad.

Sidestepping sexist slights, Tess maintained focus on a shared goal: "I learned to become a team player outside the family, realizing that if people cooperate, they can do something more. It's a thrilling thing, making something more because you are with other people, getting along basically." She went on:

I had extraordinary female mentors in all my jobs, including other female deans. When I was the dean, there were very few of us in the country. We were a very tight group. The women faculty at the law school were very excited that I was the first female dean and were incredibly supportive. The fact that I was female was appreciated.

I imagine that Tess's use of humor and cooperation also helped heal deep scars from her early emotional and physical mistreatment—productive, safe collaboration as a hopeful alternative to the "knock down drag outs" of earlier life.

Tess has arrived at a deep-seated belief in her capabilities and self-worth. Looking back, she is deeply proud of her successful professional life, knowing it was hard won. She ended our time together letting me know, "I really feel weird to sit here and talk about myself for two hours— obviously I didn't stop!" Her self-conscious sentiment was echoed by almost every woman I interviewed, poignantly contrasting with the genuine delight I felt getting to know them and myself in the process.

Chapter 11

Margot

In one of my earliest encounters with Margot, an impressive, 40-something Black trauma surgeon from a renowned urban teaching hospital on the West Coast, we tumbled into a critical enactment. Ultimately, as in the best of cases, our discussion of the disturbing event added safety and freedom to our moving interview, but not before it caused me significant embarrassment for what I had failed to address.

It all began after I emailed Margot a pre-interview questionnaire (age, demographics, etc.) and asked her to complete and return it to me in advance of our conversation. This was my protocol with all six women. But, as our interview date neared, I had not yet received Margot's completed questionnaire. As I pondered what might be involved, it only then dawned on me that I had not included any questions about race in my questionnaire. I immediately went to work adding questions and contacted Margot to say that I realized my omission about racial issues was problematic and revealed my privileged White position and implicit bias. I asked if she would allow me to send her amended questions that addressed her experiences of race early on and professionally. Margot listened and, at least outwardly, seemed to accept what I had to say, agreeing to complete an amended set of questions. In fact, I received that document back from her almost immediately. With this, I felt something open up a bit more between Margot and me; a softening, with more trust and room to move together.

I have come to believe that these difficult early moments between us made space for a more honest and trusting conversation between Margot and me, particularly regarding race. Early on in our interview, she said, "Race is always present, but I don't often think about it, because I don't know anything other than being a Black woman. It doesn't always occur to me that I am experiencing life differently from other people." But, as it turned out, race became a prominent and productive theme threaded

DOI: 10.4324/9781003476085-14

throughout our interview, illuminating many essential aspects of Margot's life and experiences.

Margot is a heterosexual, single, Black professional who grew up in the Northwest region of the United States and attended an Ivy League college. She works at the top, as the chief of the trauma service at a world-renowned Level I trauma center on the West Coast. She conducts complex emergency operations seven days a week and is intimately involved with teaching residents. She has received frequent recognition from her trainees and institution for her outstanding teaching skills and her commitment to education. With combined curiosity and awe, I wondered what combination of circumstances had birthed the moxie and intellect that I saw in Margot. Her interview reflected the precision, crispness, and focus one expects from a fine surgeon. The only characteristic that did not neatly fit this stereotype was her steadfast humility, a trait I observed in all my interviewees.

Margot's father was also a physician, and her mother was an elementary school teacher. Margot's dry sense of humor stood out from the beginning as she described her family to me:

My father wanted six sons, but instead he got four daughters. So, he raised us like sons. We are all very capable and self-sufficient and ended up in very nontraditional professions. He always said we could do whatever we wanted, even though he was a huge male chauvinist about anything besides us. He planted the seeds for all of us.

The path was wide and clear for Margot and her sisters to study and pursue their passions:

There were never gender roles in my house—this is a boy's job, this is a girl's job. In elementary school, I once had to draw a picture of my family, and I drew my dad cooking. The school called to say I had problems understanding gender roles. Not skipping a beat, my mother told the teacher, "My husband taught *me* how to cook," at which point the teacher said, "I wish mine did!"

Margot's mother offered a model of confidence and directness:

She was the only girl with four brothers, so she was much blunter than the women of her time, and she passed that on to *me,* in particular! I'm sometimes told I'm a little too abrupt, and as I've gotten older, I've learned to use a little more diplomacy.

Margot felt that she and her mother were very close but also different. Her mother was "an extreme extrovert, the cool mom on the block, and I am a self-described introvert." Despite their fundamental differences in temperament, Margot's mother showed an impressive ability early on to recognize and support her daughter. This was reflected in the way Margot knew and trusted her own instincts and moods from her earliest years:

> When she was ready to go back to work, [my mother] enrolled me in nursery school at 2-and a half, unheard of back then, and the feedback from my teacher was "she interacts very well, but she knows when she's had enough and needs to be by herself."

Margot had the benefit of early parental attunement that facilitated the development of her sturdy sense of self. When we discussed her academic interests and choice of careers, Margot said, "I knew in my mind what would and wouldn't work for me."

Margot and her mother enjoyed a loving and supportive relationship with many superficial similarities, but ultimately, "I realized how much like my Dad I was." More stoical and introverted, he grew up very poor in the deep South and became a doctor against significant odds:

> As a kid, I got tired of hearing over and over again how he struggled, until I heard my friend brag about him and say how impressive he was. Then I realized, he's kind of a big deal. In retrospect, I wish I'd spent more time talking to him about his childhood, particularly living with an abusive stepfather.

Margot's father wanted to give to his daughters boundlessly, a likely reflection of his deprived early life, but Margot is grateful that her mother felt otherwise:

> My mother would tell him, "That makes for some terrible people." So, she reined him in. She would tell us, "You've got a job and a checkbook, use it!" I'm thankful for that now. I don't have to shower myself with all sorts of stuff.

Like Mia, Margot felt that early experiences of having to work hard for what she wanted promoted growth, resilience, and positive core values, but she was also keenly aware of her privilege:

> I had some guilt about not having gone through the same struggles as others, because I never wanted for things. But I also realized that, despite all that, I still have to live with being a Black person in America.

Consistent with my other interviewees, Margot's family was deeply loving and supportive, but once again not outwardly expressive emotionally:

> It's funny, my oldest sister is always posting positive things about me; she's very proud of her little sister. But that seems weird, because my family was not very demonstrative. My mom was more demonstrative than dad, but our joke used to be we're the "S" family: we don't have feelings. You never sort of put yourself out there.

I said, "but both your parents, particularly your father, must have been so proud of you." She replied:

> He would never express it; he didn't know how to say it. Once, he gave me all his old medical books. Looking back, I can see he was saying, "welcome to my world, to those things that are so important to me, and I was worried you weren't going to be part of it," since I didn't go directly to medical school. But I missed the significance at the time. I would have preferred a record player or something like that.

In fact, all the women discussed thus far described the emotional climate of their families similarly. Charlotte, Mia, Tess, and now Margot came from environments where emotions were not discussed and expected to be tightly controlled. I continued to wonder internally about the cost of such austere procedural rules (discussed further in Chapter 16).

The taboo on emotional expression also extended to boasting of any kind. As Margot said:

> Sometimes people tell me I should be more active on Instagram. They post about their accomplishments and have big followings. But I say, why are they posting that? I've done way better cases, but it feels too

prideful to put myself out like that. I guess it has something to do with my upbringing—don't put yourself above others. Growing up, I was always very smart, at the top of my class, but my older sisters made it their job to bring me down to earth, reminding me I was nothing special.

Staying humble was a family affair. And being Black and female further cemented Margot's early learning:

My sisters and I all went into very male-dominated fields, so we were often the only woman and the only Black person in the room—it's the way we grew up. So, that's part of why I don't make a big deal about what I've done. So, when people say this person was the first Black person in their residency or fellowship, I was all those things, but I never made a point of broadcasting it. In the years when I began, anything I did, I was going to be the first. So, I just shut up and did my work.

For Margot, being humble about all she has accomplished exists in ongoing tension with her confidence and deep-seated belief about all that she offers. As with the other successful women I met, she has capitalized on early family models of hard work and resilience, and in Margot's case, the affirmative mirroring she received:

Deep inside, there's a part of me that recognizes I am not just an average Joe, and that is what drives me. I'm always surprised by how others see me, but I tell myself to think of myself that way. The other half is telling me, "Don't get puffed up about it, just see what you can do." You get the recognition, or you don't, but you don't do it for that.

Like Tess, who could see the disparity between how she felt about herself and how others viewed her, Margot resolved to incorporate a view of herself that included more, knowing at a deeper level it reflected the truth.

The reining in of emotions and negative reactions in Margot's family extended to anger and any form of outwardly aggressive behavior. Once, for a year and a half, her father refused to talk to her after she decided to defer medical school and spend two post-college years teaching:

He was so mad, he couldn't even have a conversation with me—he was convinced I would never go to medical school, even though I never thought I wouldn't. I'd always been fascinated by science, and with the exposure to my dad, it was what I wanted to do. I just needed some time; I was burned out. Once I committed to go to medical school, my dad calmed down. He said, "You probably noticed I wasn't too happy with your decision."

I told her I was impressed by her ability to hold her own at such a young age and not capitulate to her father's demands. "I knew what worked for me," she said.

As for her mother's anger, Margot said she was always controlled, but:

You knew when my mother was angry, but nobody in my house was a yeller. You didn't use the words "shut up," no slamming doors, all very controlled anger, but you knew when she was unhappy. There wasn't a lot of drama, nothing crazy going on. I would go to friends' houses where people were screaming and yelling, and I thought that was terrible.

This early modeling of controlled aggression, at least in Margot's mother, reached deep inside of her:

As a result of all this, I have a really hard time with very angry people. I find it exhausting to be around and so unlike me. Even on the street, when I hear people's angry conversations on their cell phones, my first thought is, "How can you be in public like that?" My second is, "How much energy does that take?" We were all about control the anger.

There was one notable exception to this emotionally restrained household picture:

My earliest memory was: one day, when I came home from nursery school, and I wet my pants. I, of course, was mortified, but I can't tell you how often my sisters would bring that up. It was terrible, the one thing I literally remember about nursery school. It was always three against one. I was the youngest, and they teased me mercilessly. It wasn't until we were adults that it actually became the four of us.

When I noted that this all seemed pretty mean, Margot added, "I guess that's what sisters do. I was used to their teasing and humor as disguised aggression." Whether it was her resilient constitution or otherwise positive environment, or both, Margot remembered this pain but never grew demoralized by the actions of her sisters, who, to this day, she greatly admires and loves. Maybe tolerating their teasing and even shaming emboldened her to face later professional challenges as a Black woman in a demanding work environment dominated by White men.

As a female surgeon, Margot cultivates and maintains a professional image that reflects her authority, competence, and, most importantly, her steady cool. She knows that all this becomes even more freighted when it comes to a woman, and a Black woman at that:

> The female aspect seems to be a bigger deal than the race part. The field is the patriarchy, where men think they are more qualified than the women. I've never felt it from the residents, who just want me to teach, or the nurses, who initially resist me and my style but change when they recognize my work. But definitely, I've felt it from my faculty colleagues. And when you add in the Black part, I don't have the luxury of being angry. Being pretty even-keeled has been good for me professionally because, as a Black woman, I cannot be publicly angry.

But inevitably, in such a high-stakes environment, things get difficult. Margot's steady way of addressing such moments brought to my mind her home, where anger was present though quietly managed:

> The residents know when I'm upset, because I speak differently. Very calmly, I enumerate my words, and they know when I'm not happy. I'm not yelling, not telling them to shut up. *And if I did what male colleagues do in these situations, I would be the bitch* [emphasis added]. Women suffer with being the bitch, but I also have to deal with being the angry Black woman. Talk to any Black woman in a leadership position, and they'll tell you the same thing—we don't have the luxury of being angry or even emotional. Look at Michelle Obama.

In addition to managing her anger at work, Margot's need to establish her authority is ever-present, including maintaining boundaries, not revealing anything personal, and:

> establishing yourself as the doctor. I always introduce myself as "Dr. S." I don't have the luxury of being friends with people, and I can't get away with being too chummy or revealing with the residents, like the men can. I need to show myself as a person in charge. I'm not warm and cuddly.

She continued, "In fact, I am the boss, and I like it that way!" I noted to myself what a tightrope this must be, to embody confidence, competence, and authority but never a whiff of aggression. It reminded me of what many believed about Hillary Clinton—that, regardless of how she presented herself, she would have been seen as aggressive and unlikeable, since she triggered the culture's discomfort with women who act powerfully beyond the safe boundaries of marriage and family (Zuckerman, 2019).

The administration at Margot's hospital has been recently focused on institutional racism. Although Margot appreciates this, like many others in her position, she feels it is a burden to not only be the face of diversity training as the rare Black women in leadership, but also a stand-in for her entire race:

> I appreciate the need, but it's exhausting. We call it the "Black Tax." First, you have to be exemplary in everything you do and represent. No one ever says, "We had a White male resident, and he was terrible," but they do say, "Remember the last Black guy we had, he was terrible." So, I tell all the Black residents, "You represent everybody, and you'll always be the person tagged. Like I chair our committee, so I am trotted out as the picture of diversity." Other people go to work, come home, and don't have to think about how they behave and speak. *It must be so easy to be a White man* [emphasis added].

As Margot reflected on the arc of her career, she told me she never had the benefit of mentors. "I just figured things out on my own every step of the way." But she now understands that she herself has become a vital model and influence as one of the earliest Black women in her field. Being viewed as a mentor feels odd, as she "never intended to be a pioneer. I am an 'accidental leader,' but I now see I have an aptitude for it." As an introvert, it is not easy for her to step out in front, but Margot rises to the challenge:

> I have started to speak up more with age, being much more vocal about what I've been through. I was just on a panel where I said I've seen and lived through a lot. The Black residents came up to me and thanked me. They told me they can't say it as residents, but how different their life is, how different they are treated, and how they are labeled. You have to suppress it when you're going through it, but I look back and can't believe it all. I tell them, "I am here, and you can be here, too. I did this 20 years ago, where no other people looked like me or had done similar things."

As we neared the end of our conversation, I shared with Margot how moved I was that she had been so open and real with me. Her frankness and vulnerability added richness and dimensionality to being with her. She invited me into her world, its challenges, and how stunningly resilient and focused she has been. As she says it best:

If you're a person who's going to rise to the top, you do what it takes to rise to the top. You have to do more of it, because you don't have the backing from a spouse or mentors. That would be the biggest thing I've felt in my life, but you do it anyway. One nice thing I can say about being a surgeon: if you're competent, nobody cares about anything else. The minute you prove your competence, you're done, you're fine. Unless, of course, you go somewhere else, and then you'll have to prove it all over again—as a woman, that is.

Chapter 12

Sandra

Sandra is a 60-something, White, heterosexual attorney who rose to become a U.S. magistrate judge, the first female federal officer of the judiciary in her state. She strikes me as wise, accomplished, and reflective about who she is and how she got there, a perfect candidate for our interview. Sandra told me that she pondered my interview questions and talked them through with family members well in advance of our meeting, evidencing her seriousness of purpose and preparedness. Early on in our conversation, she interrupted herself to say it felt strange to talk about herself for this amount of time, yet it was obvious to me that she was also embracing the opportunity fully. "Are my stories boring? I don't know, I just know I'm totally engaged with the stories I'm telling you." I told Sandra I felt honored to know her and learn a bit about who she is.

Sandra grew up middle class in the Mid-Atlantic region of the United States. She now resides in the East and is widowed. Despite always being an outstanding student, she envisioned only a stereotypically female future for herself early on:

> I understood I had two choices: nurse or teacher. Although I leaned toward nursing, my family and friends said I was more verbal than caretaker, so I chose teaching. Only the upheaval of the 1960s caused me to see other possibilities and eventually attend law school.

Dale Evans and Annie Oakley were Sandra's early heroines, and, after telling me she practiced target shot with an Annie Oakley long gun, she quipped, "Early aggression?" We chuckled together, and I assured her she was on to something, appreciating her clever sense of humor and her willingness to be playful with our subject matter. Sandra participated in

DOI: 10.4324/9781003476085-15

numerous extracurricular activities during her school years, but one was transformational:

> In those years, I was devoted to my horses. I rode and showed in local shows when we could afford it, I had a registered quarter horse, plus worked at a stable. The horses were really important in my early life. I was responsible for feeding, caring, exercising, and training them. I worked long hours and developed a sense of responsibility and respect for animals. I think those horses were essential in making me the person that I am.

A horse lover myself, I was delighted to learn about Sandra's inspirational experiences with horses as we spoke together about our mutual early love for Walter Farley's *Black Stallion* book series for children. And, as with Charlotte, Mia, Margot, and Tess, I noted Sandra's appreciation for how early hard work and responsibility installed an invaluable work ethic that has carried her through life. But, in addition to all this, Sandra told me that her most inspirational model of all was her maternal grandmother, Nanny:

> Nanny was a widow and bookkeeper who stayed with us on weekends, eventually retired, and moved in when I was 10. As my primary care-taker, her life lesson was: "Make sure you have your own income and independence, because you can't depend on a man—even the best of them could up and die on you."

Reflecting her internalization of Nanny, Sandra added, "I pictured myself growing up to be strong and independent, and in fact *became* strong and independent-minded." I could feel it in Sandra. She did not seem burdened by the need to take care of me during our time together, or compelled to sti-fle her disagreement when I shared my inferences about things she had said. She simply stated her difference of opinion respectfully after considering my input in a serious, free-thinking way.

After tossing around my interview questions with her,[1] Sandra's daughter insisted that she share this essential story with me:

> She said, "Make sure you tell her about Nanny and the shoes. That's your role model!" So, up until a week before she died, my grandmother used to wear those black, lace-up Oxford shoes of the fifties. And every

morning, she got down on the floor and put on her shoes when she got dressed. That was the ritual, down on the floor, shoes on, make your bed, and get going. Apparently, that stuck with my daughter, since I've told that story so many times.

Sandra felt loved by her parents, grandmother, great aunt, and uncle, though "I don't remember them ever telling me they loved me per se. They weren't demonstrative, but they were always proud when I did well in school or in anything and told me I was special in many ways." Because she was an only child, "I played with kids in the neighborhood during the day, but evenings, weekends, and holidays were with this cohort. They were my people." Paralleling the early environments of all my interviewees, Sandra's family was not outwardly expressive about emotions. But, given the way she presented herself, it seemed apparent that the message of feeling valued and deeply loved came through in other ways.

Sandra's mother was a high school English teacher, and her father was a steel mill worker who eventually owned his own home remodeling and construction business. He built the home Sandra lived in for most of her childhood. Sandra never felt very close to her father, who she referred to by his first name. "He was independent in the household, and we shared a difficult personal history after my mother died." It was then that her father remarried "the wicked, alcoholic stepmother," who was not much older than Sandra.

Eventually, her father became ill with cancer and, as he was dying and divorcing his second wife, he went to live with Sandra. "We reconciled then, I guess, but he never apologized for the worst thing he did toward my daughter." While visiting her in college, Sandra's father bribed Sandra's daughter with cash and manipulated her to sign over savings bonds that had been gifted to her by Sandra's parents. This was all for the purpose of taking his second wife to Florida. Sandra told her father that he was lucky she was not pressing charges against him, and for an entire year they did not speak, until she was forced to bail him out of jail following a domestic dispute.

Despite her manifest shame and anger over these episodes, Sandra repeatedly took pains to remind me, "I owed my father big time for taking care of my mother . . . I never was any help." Her impressive ability to hold in tension the many contradictory sides of her father echoed further in the following:

> The law has taught me that you have to be able to see both sides of everything. You wind up worrying: Am I turning into a mush? . . . So, it's frustrating . . . but I like thinking that way, stopping and saying, wait a minute, what's the countervailing argument, and how does it compare to what I'm saying?

Though set within a legal rather than psychological framework, we can nonetheless feel Sandra's commitment to experiencing the world from multiple perspectives with the whole object in mind, ways of being that are woven through who she is.

Sandra originally pursued a career as a college English professor but discovered early on that she hated graduate school and taught high school instead for several years before returning to law school. She has worked in numerous legal capacities as a state prosecutor, district attorney, state district court judge, justice of the superior court, and ultimately the first female officer of the federal judiciary in her state, as a U.S. magistrate judge.[2] Reflecting upon different aspects of her career, Sandra noted:

> I like my work and find the law interesting. I like having a job where I'm the decision maker; versus teaching, where I felt bound by the curriculum, administrators, and public school atmosphere. As a state court judge, I liked least sentencing people to very long periods behind bars and the heart-wrenching work of awarding child custody to one parent over the other, or worse, placing a child in state custody. I went to the federal courts to get away from discretionary sentencing and child custody cases.

She said that "obnoxious litigants and tight deadlines" were among the most stressful parts of her job, then clued me in to a critical component of how she handles aggression:

> In coping with these stressors, I always try to practice rule number one of judge's school: "Never say or do anything when you're upset with the person in front of you." You are the judge, and you can take a recess. Better to call a recess than call the litigant by a name or make a fool of yourself. . . . When you're angry, you're out of control, and that's not a

good thing for a judge. That's something you work on. I was appointed to teach judge school, a three-week summer program for new judges to learn about legal substance and judicial temperament. There are classes with psychiatrists and psychologists on implicit bias and judicial temperament.

Sandra then spoke about how she learned early on to be aware of her anger, to control it, and to transform it into something constructive:

Anger was suppressed in me because of showing and training my horse. You can't be angry when you're dealing with animals, even when they make you angry. You always have to breathe and deal with it in some kind of way other than losing it, which doesn't move you forward. This is where I first learned emotional control, which to me is power.

Her practical, controlled approach to her aggression proved critical to her later success:

My husband maintained that I got where I did professionally by being one of the boys. Not partying but by making sure to go out for lunch and talk about cases. *And if I disagreed with their positions, I did it in a very low-key manner* [emphasis added]. For example, one of my mentors maintained that, as a prosecutor, you never wanted women on a rape jury, because they would judge the woman more harshly than a man. We talked about that a great deal, and, while I felt it could be true in some cases, it wasn't a rule of thumb. He and I found a middle ground. *I used my aggression by being stubborn and sticking to the issues without being irate* [emphasis added].

I immediately added, "That's the goal!" Sandra laughed and seemed to appreciate my resonance with how she had found creative strategies to position her aggression safely and usefully.

Of course, as a judge, things did not always roll out smoothly, but, in moments of conflict, Sandra's skill and faith in the process of repair added to her success:

As for deadlines, my staff would probably say I didn't cope well. I was compulsive about getting things done on time, and *I could get, I'm afraid to say, sort of nasty* [emphasis added]. However, in my chambers, we always have a cuppa at 3 pm to talk over cases and shoot the breeze.

It was time well spent, because we would discuss how soon an opinion would be ready *and make up for my bad behavior* [emphasis added]. Teatime was always a stress releaser.

That said, Sandra does harbor some regrets:

I didn't get along with the head clerk of the federal courts because of how poorly she treated staff. My administrative assistant told me the clerk was envious, because I was an attorney and she wasn't, but she made me so angry I . . . wanted to smack her! I'm too sensitive to say it didn't hurt my feelings, but, even though she was so obnoxious, I still felt I could have worked through it. Instead, I stopped talking to her. . . . One of the male judges had the same problem with her, but he used to be brutal to her. He got away with it. *As long as they get the paperwork done on time, the males don't pay attention to these things* [emphasis added].

I agreed with her observation about her male colleagues, noting that, as the dominant group, men are often blind to their privilege and inherent sexism. I also shared that our culture typically dubs women the relationship care-takers (as described in Part I), which leaves Sandra feeling regret over not working things through with the clerk, whereas her male colleague can "be brutal . . . and get away with it." His aggression is culturally forgiven, even valued. Given this cultural inequity, I particularly enjoyed Sandra's comfort with her own aggression when she announced, "I . . . wanted to smack her!," referring to the head clerk she tangled with.

Our discussion of the sociocultural barriers to women's aggression easily led us to Sandra's views and experiences with patriarchy:

Here's a story I don't share with everyone. After the governor appointed me state court judge, he called me to his office with the attorney general to discuss my upcoming confirmation hearing. He said, "The chairman of the committee is going to vote against you, because you have a different last name from your husband." He [the governor] advised me to keep my mouth shut and be polite, because this guy would never say this publicly, and members of the opposing party were on my side. This fried me, because two weeks earlier, this same guy voted to confirm my male friend who was married to a woman with a different last name! I knew it wasn't fair, but that's how I deal with my anger—smile and go with the flow. The best thing afterwards was when the law school dean wrote me and said, "It's nice you became judge, but it says even more about you that you got a negative vote from this guy." The dean didn't even know the inside story. He just knew this character.

I commented that Sandra was lucky that the committee chairman's misogyny did not end up hurting her. She replied:

But it shows you what is always out there. When I was pregnant, I asked my obstetrician for a pediatrician who wouldn't blame it on my work when my child had tonsillitis. She gave me someone wonderful who remained my daughter's doctor through college. I have that kind of antennae, and I deal with it. If you're always haranguing about it, it's not going to move you forward, professionally or personally. There are ways to work through it.

As for the legal profession, Sandra added,

Despite the existence of so many more women, it's a male-dominated profession at the top, really, just an extension of the larger world, which you learn is male-dominated once you're an adult. I was fortunate to work with a very enlightened judiciary, a more supportive male-dominated world.

Sandra, like every other woman with whom I spoke, showed a keen awareness of lurking patriarchal forces but exhibited a studied effort to deal with them strategically and never let them stop her. As she stated, "There are ways to work through it," a rallying cry for all the women I was interviewing (further discussed in Chapter 16).

Responding to my question about personal and professional setbacks, Sandra's resilience punctuated every example, whether about losing in a horse show, having her decision overturned by a higher court, being overweight as a child, or learning to ride a bicycle:

Don't laugh, but I probably had a harder time than any kid in America learning to ride a bicycle. But I kept after it, and, to this day, I ride ten miles a day no matter what. My dad would run beside me, push me down a hill. I'd fall over and get up and try again. In law school . . . I wasn't the best in the class anymore, but that helped me, because I've internalized you don't have to be the smartest person in the world, and even if you think you are, you may not be. If I don't learn from my setbacks, I'm really in trouble.

As our ending time drew near, I thought about how Sandra's sense of self is a testimonial to her beloved Nanny, with whom "You just didn't mess; she was all business." Sandra's self-confidence is solidly anchored but also realistic. On the one hand, she seemed to have momentarily considered scaling the highest heights. "Although I seem to fit the age demographic, I don't have presidential aspirations as . . . young people should be running this country." On the other hand, after winning a statewide speech contest in high school and being compared by the press to Indira Gandhi, she noted, "It was a bit of a reach, if you ask me." On a similarly humble note, she ended our time this way: "So, I engaged myself. It's nice to have somebody listen to my story, and I'm honored and surprised you were given my name. There are many other powerful women in higher positions who are more outspoken on feminist issues." I was moved by Sandra's humility, as well as her full presence, as we delved deeply into the events and influences that have shaped her impressive life. I had no trouble adding, "You fit the bill to a tee; it is an honor to hear your story, and I also enjoyed meeting another *Black Stallion* lover on top of it all!"

Notes

1 All interview questions were sent to interviewees prior to our meeting.
2 Magistrate judges are U.S. federal district court judges appointed through a merit selection process for renewable eight-year terms.

Chapter 13

Shirley

As with our first meetings in the consulting room, my earliest contacts with Shirley revealed much about her character and the way she meets life; in this case with a bountiful curiosity and an intense desire to self-expand. "I'm kind of a scavenger. Almost everyone I interact with is a mentor. Everyone I talk to, I learn from and take whatever I can get." It was true with us from the earliest moments:

> Your initial questionnaire was difficult and made me realize something very interesting for the first time. I'm an immigrant from Israel, and my professional life as a scientist started here in the United States, a very different cultural and emotional part of my life. Earlier, I played the piano, acted, and aspired to be a musician. So, I tried to remember the Israeli music world back then to come up with role models, but it was hard. I didn't think it would be so difficult to try to link my early childhood and where I am now, but being an immigrant was part of this equation, I now realize.

Shirley is a White, 60ish, married, heterosexual professional with two daughters. She grew up middle class in Israel and attended an Israeli university. She has two older sisters, a father who was a biochemist, and a mother who was a homemaker. Shirley immigrated to the United States in her early twenties to pursue a doctorate in microbiology, after which she headed a research group at her university and became the chair of her department. Shirley is currently the chief technology officer of one of the foremost biomedical research institutes in the United States. She is responsible for integrating business needs and research requirements into IT planning and operations. As the institute's principal strategist, she oversees its entire research enterprise.

DOI: 10.4324/9781003476085-16

Reflecting upon her early childhood, Shirley told me:

The older I get, the more I realize that my formative years in Israel have 100 percent influenced my take on life . . . both the time and place where I grew up, and my own personal family background. . . . Israel is a heterogeneous society whose hierarchy and education system are merit-based. You are judged on objective rather than subjective qualities, and, if you're not the best at everything, it's okay. This breeds humility, which is critical for those in leadership positions. In contrast, one of my daughters won prizes in her elementary school for everything, so she thinks she "walks on water." Similarly, if I tell anyone on my team they're less than perfect, there's a revolution.

Like many others I interviewed, Shirley believes that the direct, honest feedback and humility prized by her early environment, in this case Israel, were critical underpinnings of her professional ethos and success. These values anchored her, deeply instilling the importance of hard work, perseverance, and resilience. Shirley continued with a moving description of how her parents also shaped fundamental parts of who she is and how she sees the world:

Then there's the influence of my parents, who survived the Holocaust and, like many, came from Eastern Europe to Israel. My parents spared me their horror stories, but their experiences were very much part of the culture at home. I learned that you can't take anything for granted and shouldn't complain about minuscule things. . . . So, you grow up without a sense of entitlement, just grateful for the little things. It was very special. It's better to learn how to prioritize problems early in life.

As I absorbed the intensity of Shirley's message, I asked if she ever felt she had to minimize her disappointments, given what she knew her parents had endured in the War. "It's just a matter of degree," she said:

You want to get it out of your system, but you want to put it in perspective. I actually resisted, until two or three years ago, going to the concentration camps. But, after I did, it was clear I hadn't even begun to internalize what had happened. Now I say to every person I meet, you have to go, because doing so is critical to understand things that no one can even imagine humanity can become or can happen.

Shirley told me that her parents modeled mutual love and respect, even though her father led a professional life and her mother stayed home:

They really loved each other, there were difficulties, but his face brightened whenever he saw her. It was the same message: just be happy with what you have. By the way, going through these memories with you is really quite special for me.

Shifting from her earliest years, Shirley added in another uniquely defining dimension of her life:

The military is the unique thing that defines me and so many other Israelis who ascend to leadership positions. It's very easy for someone who becomes in charge to think they [sic] are in control, but military training is about the idea that, as an individual, you can't be in control. . . . For two years, all my training was group activities: what happens if this occurs, who should you look at, how you should run together? And the other amazing thing is the military is a social homogenizer. When they say I have to run, I have to, even if it's coming from someone who didn't finish high school. So, regarding issues of power and hierarchy, you're coming to it from a completely different mindset. Thinking about my own background, it doesn't matter that I have the title "executive" behind my name. . . . I need the people on the bus to run with me. I can't do it without them.

I asked Shirley if she feels women have an easier time with team building than men, who may be more competitive and ego-driven, as demanded by our culture. She granted that this may be possible in the abstract, but she feels that women have other problems working in teams:

A woman who's trying to put together a team must be hyper-focused, and, although they [sic] may tend to be more inclusive . . . they [sic] may be compromised by other things . . . their need to make everybody feel good about themselves. But team building is not about pleasing everyone, right? I think women in leadership who are charged with building teams have to change a bit the way they're thinking about what team means.

I questioned if she was referring specifically to giving people negative feedback, being straight with them, the kind of thing she explained was so different and helpful in Israel. Agreeing, she explained that her guiding principle, with any job she has held, has been 100 percent transparency:

> When you have a totally transparent system, everybody knows the expectations. So, it's easier to deliver not-so-good messages, because it's not about the person . . . it's about the job. And that's very unfortunate for women, because it takes so much effort for them to reach these kinds of positions. So, ultimately, they take it very personally.

In other words, because it is so difficult for women to reach significant leadership positions, they often end up viewing their work as synonymous with who they are, taking feedback personally, and neglecting other aspects of their lives. Alternatively, Shirley feels the job is just the job; she is going to just get it done and not be preoccupied or slowed down by what anyone else thinks of her.

Shirley's no-nonsense practicality, hyper-focus on results, and drive reminded me of others I had interviewed: Charlotte the U.S. attorney and Margot the surgeon, whose professions generally demand a more pragmatic, direct, and assertive style with little room or time for coddling or over-thinking:

> People ask me why I rarely get upset . . . because I accept the fact that sometimes things happen the way you want them to, and sometimes, they don't. Spending emotional energy on little things is a waste. To help individuals who come to my office expressing frustration about something, I remind them of the importance of having a broader perspective. I ask them to think about the real possibility of getting, at any moment, a call from a dear friend letting them know they have been diagnosed with a terminal disease. . . . Their frustration melts away.

Shirley then showed me her attitude in action:

> There's a person at work who's very talented and came to discuss a new position I was proposing for her. She demanded a title and a raise, because a man she knew had just gotten one. Offended, I said, "End of story. Let's move forward. Tell me instead one big thing that we need in this organization and tell me how you're going to do it in three years." She got it. It's about a meritocracy.

Though impressed by her clarity and focus, I could not help but ask, "But what about women who are perfectly well suited to the job but are held back unfairly by the patriarchy?" She added:

> As you point out, there are lots of cultural and sociocultural barriers for women who try to promote themselves. That's why it's critical for women to have male mentors, since the world isn't becoming equal anytime soon, and women have to learn how to interact. We can't come to the table as victims; that doesn't help, and we can't compensate by being super aggressive or super demanding. There's something not right about the way we're prepping women for leadership.

Shirley, along with all others I interviewed, believes that emphasizing female victimhood or adopting an overly aggressive style are highly ineffective tools to silence the patriarchy and get ahead. These women accept its reality but are determined to work around it and carve out a personal style that succeeds without alienating others. Shirley further explained why she believes male mentorship, direct and focused, is critical to help women:

> When I have a conversation, it's usually men I gain more from, as opposed to the "noisy" nature of the way women convey their message. Look at this interview, right? If you were conducting it with a man, he would probably have looked at the questions beforehand, jotted down some answers, and you'd be able to march right through the questions. But at the end of this conversation, you're going to have to re-listen to what we've talked about and figure out how to make some sense of the barrage of things I've shared with you. It's kind of similar. When I speak about mentorship, I say you need to have soundbites that people can take with them and digest.

I added:

> It's funny, for me, I love the tenor of *this* interview, which feels more personal, reflective, and subjective, without knowing exactly where we'll be going. Maybe the norms of exactitude, objectivity, and speed in the scientific world have a lot to do with your perspective.

In response, Shirley shared her belief that, since most people are not trained listeners as psychoanalysts are, they require the scaled-down soundbites more typical of male conversations for their communication to be effective. Her approach is to be consistently clear and efficient, with a premium placed on wasting little time and energy to reach her destination. I was reminded that she had asked her administrative assistant to work with me to select a time for our interview (the only woman who had). I imagined she thought this would be the most efficient way to proceed given our mutually demanding schedules, and no doubt she was correct. It was not hard to understand how Shirley's intense focus and drive have helped her rise to the top.

As with others I interviewed, however, Shirley herself never dreamed of becoming a leader or assuming a position of power such as she has. "I never aspired to be a leader, never asked for a leadership position. The only thing I can say about myself is that everything I do, I always try to do the best job I can." I added, "Many successful women feel surprised that they have achieved leadership, in part because there's so little cultural training for women to become leaders or to self-assert." Shirley quickly corrected me:

> Clarifying, I was not *surprised* it happened. I saw it coming in every leadership position I had, but I was not the one going after it. One way of making your leadership question more informative is to ask what kinds of characteristics one needs to assume any kind of leadership.

As her self-confidence and focused approach again emerged, I thanked Shirley for both her clarification and her input. I was impressed at her comfort refining my response and volunteering a way to improve my questionnaire, both shared in a way that managed to be direct, helpful, and collaborative at the same time. She was unburdened by the need for me to like her, exactly as she had espoused throughout our interview.

Shirley and I ended our conversation with her reflection, by now a familiar refrain to me: "It's weird for me to have a conversation when I'm doing 100 percent of the talking! I'd love to set up a time to hear your story, the fact that you decided to change careers." I thanked her and said it would be my pleasure to do so. And, knitting our time back to the beginning, she added, "I would love to; I told you every story is a mentorship opportunity for me." As confident, poised, and direct as Shirley is, it can still feel strange for a woman to occupy center stage for that long a stretch.

Chapter 14

Conversations in Context

The Literature

I now turn to the psychoanalytic literature to place these six rich interviews in their appropriate context. I discussed the literature as it relates to women's overall difficulties with self-assertion and aggression in Part I of this book, including their developmental challenges and the problem of patriarchy. At this point, I will explore those areas of the literature that speak more specifically to the barriers women face in exercising their leadership and authority.

Maccoby's (2021) long-term, cross-cultural studies on leadership are built upon the work of Freud, Fromm, and Erikson, but the author is quick to point out that none of these three psychoanalytic giants wrote about female leaders. Although women leaders in business and government were rare at the time, Anna Freud, Melanie Klein, Karen Horney, and Clara Thompson did stand out as pioneers in psychoanalysis.[1] As such, their exclusion from such important contributions on leadership reflects the way that the male-dominated psychoanalytic culture at the time generally marginalized, patronized, and oppressed women, limiting the characteristics deemed to be acceptable for those in positions of power (D'Ercole, 2023).[2] This subjugation of women was in addition to the known dangers of anyone dissenting from Freud.

Culture has certainly evolved since those times, and women leaders are now in greater supply across multiple domains, but it remains well established that women encounter an unforgiving dominant socioculture when they behave as leaders do, with aggressiveness, self-assertion, and power (Barth, 2018; Crastnopol, 2018; Eagly, 2020; Harris, 2002; Simmons, 2002; Turkel, 2000).

This minefield of patriarchal forces becomes even harsher when applied to Black women in positions of authority, such as Vice President Kamala Harris and U.S. Supreme Court Justice Ketanji Brown Jackson. They have

DOI: 10.4324/9781003476085-17

been regularly subjected to intense slurs and smears and are continually forced to navigate the "double jeopardy" of gender and racial discrimination. That is, the social environment expects them to be angry and unconsciously selects for it (Campbell, 1993; Obama, 2018; Simmons, 2002; Traister, 2018; Williams & Dempsey, 2014), reacts more harshly toward mistakes on the job where "any imperfection can be inflated into a fundamental flaw" (Blow, 2024), and insists that they prove themselves again and again (Eagly, 2020; Williams & Dempsey, 2014).

Additional gender stereotypes related to diverse cultural identities include assertiveness/strength and greater masculinity for both African American women (the "strong Black woman")[3] and lesbians, labels that grant these groups more freedom to be assertive than White women (Williams & Dempsey, 2014); intelligence and "forever foreign" for Asian American women (Williams & Dempsey, 2014); and communality for White women (Eagly, 2020).

The cultural vehicles that undercut women's achievement in the work environment are legion. They include (1) holding women to higher standards and proof of competence than men, (2) expecting their behaviors and contributions to represent their entire gender (Ganesan, 2016; Williams & Dempsey, 2014),[4] (3) treating them as if they are invisible (Turkle, 2021), (4) speaking over and interrupting them, and (5) allowing powerful others to co-opt their contributions (Liptak, 2017; Phillips, 2015; Williams & Dempsey, 2014).

As previously noted, one of the most pernicious and entrenched gender stereotypes is the expectation that women are inherently communal and men are inherently agentic, a false attribution that trails women closely in their working worlds. Like all such gendered stereotypes, it is laid down in infancy (or before), acting as a powerful filter through which all human interaction is interpreted (Williams & Dempsey, 2014). It is so deeply embedded in the patriarchy that it not only tenaciously persists but is also passed off as part of nature (even God-given) by women and men alike (Millett, 1970). All such faulty blueprints intentionally bypass the reality that our definitions of masculinity and femininity are always time-bound and independent of biological sex (Williams & Dempsey, 2014), and that women have made vast changes in their societal roles and workplace participation (Ben-Noam, 2018; Eagly, 2020; Frankel, 2015; Maccoby, 2021; Reciniello, 2011; Zuckerman, 2019).[5] We thus allow ourselves to stay blind to the cultural forces that encode such gendered scripts, penalizing women who point them out (Grant, 2023) and reinforcing the predictability, comfort, and normalcy gained by unconsciously perpetuating an unequal status quo (Zuckerman, 2019).

As described in Chapter 5, it was patriarchal forces dating all the way back to ancient times (Beard, 2017) that ensconced the male voice as the ultimate symbol of morality, law, and authority. Shockingly, we continue to unconsciously discriminate against the female voice,[6] affording men a presumption of legitimacy and stereotyping success as male. Women are warned to remain silent and polite (Eagly, 2020; Williams & Dempsey, 2014) and to move aside, allowing male voices to dominate.

These malignant tropes are held securely in place by numerous discriminatory forces: (1) minimizing and discriminating against prominent women in public leadership roles; (2) maintaining a dual classification system that interprets the same behavior favorably for men but unfavorably for women; (3) maintaining the illusion that men are more serious, competent workers (Williams & Dempsey, 2014); and (4) casting women as frightening, nasty, bitchy, and "other" when they take command (Wolf, 2021).

The female leader is thus faced with an impossible dilemma—to be a credible authority figure she must be dominant and loud; yet, as a woman, she will be negatively judged for assuming these very qualities (Eagly, 2020; Phillips, 2015). As described in Chapter 2, I lived this destabilizing clash in my prior work as a litigating attorney, where I felt the need to be fierce and fearless as a successful professional but passive and likeable as a successful woman, a no-win trap that I failed to escape.

As a result, women aspiring to leadership positions must be strategic in the face of this impossibility. They may soften their approach by various means: trying to be more democratic and collaborative; seeking consensus; delaying decisions; and using "tentative language,"[7] all to avoid criticism that they are overly authoritative and bossy (Ben-Noam, 2018; Eagly, 2020; Reciniello, 2011). Male leaders, in contrast, have cultural permission to be more autocratic and directive. (Later in this chapter, I describe my reliance upon many of these tactics as the leader of my psychoanalytic institute.) Women's reliance on these softening strategies, however, can sometimes backfire by weakening public confidence in their capacity to be effective leaders (Frankel, 2015).

Maccoby (2021) cautions us not to overly generalize about leadership styles and to remain aware of the context surrounding the female leader, since notable female heads of state have often differed in their leadership approaches. For example, more contemporary leaders, such as Angela

Merkel of Germany, Jacinda Ardern of New Zealand, and Sanna Marin of Finland, relied on a more collaborative leadership style during the COVID-19 pandemic, and notably achieved greater consensus and results than many male heads of state. However, earlier leaders like Margaret Thatcher, Golda Meir, and Indira Gandhi were known as tough and domineering, at a time when far fewer women were visible leaders and collaboration was less culturally acceptable for an authority figure than it is today. Although these earlier leaders had little choice in their leadership style given the prevailing social conditions, they were nonetheless judged harshly for their reliance on traditionally male behavior: "Attila the Hen," "the only man in her cabinet," and the "old witch," respectively (Ben-Noam, 2018).

As many have noted (Chodorow, 1978, 1995; Reciniello, 2011; Sandberg, 2013; Zuckerman, 2019), it is not only this misogynistic cultural landscape that sabotages women's achievement to sustain existing power inequities, but as well its intersection with women's co-existing intrapsychic conflicts. "The intrapsychic dynamics of individuality, selfhood and gender-sexuality [are tied] to the sociology, political economy and culture of gender" (Bueskens, 2021, p. 54). This powerful amalgam of external and internal forces installs and locks in gender hierarchies along with those of race, class, and sexuality, and mandates "correct" social identities for girls that coalesce in adolescence, and for boys around kindergarten (Gilligan, 2004). For girls, these identities must include: (1) caretaking their relationships and attuning first to the needs of others (Feldt, 2014); (2) modesty (Phillips, 2015; Williams & Dempsey, 2014); and (3) splitting off essential dimensions of themselves, such as agency, autonomy, and independence. Boys, in parallel, are pressured to split off their dependency, vulnerability, and emotionality and are later penalized for showing it (Grant, 2023).

Any violation of these scripts by girls risks the loss of vital social connections, including parental love, along with a rush of extreme guilt (Reciniello, 2011). As such, girls comply by (1) silencing themselves and minimizing their achievements (Gilligan, 1982; Phillips, 2015; Sandberg, 2010, 2013), (2) striving for perfection, (3) foregoing competition, and (4) trying to fit in. The nice girls who live out these childhood messages will be poorly suited to assume and execute leadership positions powerfully and effectively (Frankel, 2015). Ultimately, anchoring these conventional and unequal gender identities remains an unfortunate though consistent priority for most parents. They, too, are captives of a patriarchal culture (Layton, 2020) that pressures women to squander their potential, and prompts an unconscious rage that is transmitted intergenerationally in unmodulated, unusable forms (Campbell, 1993; Harris, 1997; Turkel, 2000).

Parents and other important caregivers who, in contrast, are able to actively resist these cultural norms and live more comfortably with their own affects and aggression (Winnicott, 1965, 1969) will be better suited to offer their daughters the essential attunement that fosters emotional regulation and constructive aggression (Coates, 1998; Ganesan, 2016; Knox, 2013; Layton, 2020; Pizer, 2003; Reckling & Buirski, 1996; Zuckerman, 2019). Early identification with such parental figures also offers protection against internalized misogyny and transferential distortions from outside figures that will always accompany women in leadership positions (Wolf, 2021). As an example, during my tenure as director of my psychoanalytic institute (further detailed below), I often felt that I was viewed as an entirely different person than the one I had been before assuming the helm.

Importantly, studies of female leaders cross-culturally reveal striking similarities in their early development despite vast cultural and political differences (Ganesan, 2016). One such study, in China and the UAE from 2009 to 2010,[8] found that all women described finding their voices at family dinner-table conversations, where their reactions and opinions were invited and valued even when divergent. The women particularly emphasized the role of their fathers, who encouraged them to speak up and introduced them to books from their foreign travels. Interviews with female leaders in Uganda, Tunisia, and India (Ganesan, 2016) similarly revealed that family environments, and specifically fathers, empowered them to learn, ask questions, and form opinions, rather than prioritize marrying well. Mothers who transcended cultural stereotypes by displaying leadership qualities and returning to school were also felt to be pivotal.

Other studies of female achievers in America confirmed that women's formative ties were to their fathers, who attended to their needs for nurturance but also unsettled patriarchal norms by fostering their empowerment and growth (Sageman, 2004). In all these studies, the role of attentive and involved fathers proved to be uniquely potentiating.

As a note of caution, some have observed that, even when women do achieve notable positions of leadership, they may end up overvaluing their jobs given the difficulty of attaining them. This dynamic can make it difficult for them to accept feedback and tolerate criticism in their only felt place of value (Reynolds, 2015). My interviewee, Shirley, spoke about this self-thwarting dynamic often seen in her mentees (see Chapter 13).

Strategies to Address the Problem

Returning now to my original area of inquiry, how is it that some women manage to successfully circumvent the powerful social forces that block them from positions of authority and influence? What combination of personal strategies and improved social conditions has allowed more of them to have a seat at the table?

One dimension of this important question relates to a significant cultural transformation taking place as more women reach visible seats of power, and it is no longer as strange to see them in charge (Eagly, 2020; Regine, 2015; Wolf, 2021). This shift incorporates an updated vision of leadership that is more collaborative, democratic, interactive, and less dominating. It leans on so-called feminine skills that have been historically devalued by the patriarchy—inclusiveness, connectedness, empathy, deep listening, bridge building, relational intelligence—and elevates them to the very skills required for effective leadership (Feldt, 2014; Frankel, 2015; Rhode & Kellerman, 2007). One vivid example of this new paradigm is the three female founders of the political and social movement, Black Lives Matter, who describe themselves as a leaderless group of "simply people in the community who are saying change must occur" (Crosby & Edwards, 2021, p. 515).[9] Another example of this new leadership paradigm is the growing prevalence of male partners who are stepping back to support their rising female partners, such as Vice President Kamala Harris's husband, Doug Emhoff, who "took a sledgehammer to toxic masculinity" (Caperhart, 2023), and the partners of Justices Sandra Day O'Connor and Ruth Bader Ginsburg.

In this reimagined portrait of leadership, the feminine is not owned by any gender (Pittinsky et al., 2007; Wolf, 2021), is innate in young boys and girls (though later sacrificed by men), and includes critical features possessed by both women and men. It is perceived to be as strong and powerful as the masculine and uses power for and with others, rather than over them (Regine, 2015; Wolf, 2021).[10]

It is interesting to observe that, as the dominant culture recalibrates to accommodate rising female leaders, the very meaning of the word "leadership" has been transfigured to include a collaborative dimension that is perceived to be intrinsic to women leaders. But ironically, the reliance of women leaders upon a more interactive style, in reality, reflects their proven need to eschew direct expressions of aggression, rather than a way of being that is original or innate in women. As such, the shift in meaning of the word "leadership" adds an updated and more democratic element to the concept, but it also ends up calcifying an erroneous cultural stereotype—that women leaders are inherently more communal than men (see above; and note 11 of this Chapter, describing how reliance upon notions of androgyny perpetuates damaging stereotypes).

That said, many continue to maintain that the best path forward for today's female leaders is an integration of both female qualities emphasizing relationality and male qualities emphasizing strength—an amalgam of agentic and communal characteristics that shifts toward androgyny (Eagly, 2020; Johnson et al., 2008; Reciniello, 2015), while maintaining a watchful eye on how anger is expressed. In other words, combining warmth with dominance and communality with competence is thought to be the most effective approach for today's female leaders. Notably, men need only show agency without incorporating warmth (Johnson et al., 2008). As Slaughter puts it:

> The continued theme . . . is balance: balance between masculine and feminine, principle and pragmatism, niceness and authority, self-promotion and selflessness, and work and family. . . . We will not succeed if we approach our lives angry and embittered. So, we must balance awareness and activism with getting it done as professionally as we know how.[11]
>
> (Williams & Dempsey, 2014, p. xvii)

We can find powerful examples of this new leadership formula among many of today's outstanding female leaders, attesting to its efficacy for the current sociopolitical moment. In the political sphere, three political giants who recently died—Sandra Day O'Connor, Ruth Bader Ginsburg, and Diane Feinstein—embodied many of its core ingredients. Sandra Day O'Connor understood that she would be more powerful, not less, by embodying self-restraint and civility. She never showed off or carried grudges (Thomas, 2023), just moved on, and got it done (VanSickle, 2023). Ruth Bader Ginsburg humbly attributed her success to being in the right place with the right arguments at the right time (Greenhouse, 2020). And Diane Feinstein acknowledged the patriarchy but continued on with what she thought was right (Dowd, 2023a) and always emphasized resiliency: "We all suffer defeat . . . and we have to be like the phoenix and rise again" (Fahy, 2023, para. 11).

As well, Nancy Pelosi, the first woman to be elected speaker of the U.S. House of Representatives, called upon a mixed-gender leadership style, as seen by her resilience in quietly weathering sustained personal attacks from conservatives, brutally pragmatic focus (Cottle, 2022) on getting things done, intense work ethic, humility toward her own innovations, and refusal to blame others for her setbacks. And, in a powerful reversal of meanings that many women leaders employ, Pelosi flipped "that whole grandmother-in-pearls thing" (Cottle, 2022, para. 5) to her competitive advantage by lulling others into believing she could be easily outmaneuvered or intimidated, when that was anything but the case (Cottle, 2022).

One final example in the academic world of a contemporary female leader who deftly combines relationality with strength is Dartmouth College's Jewish studies chair, Susannah Heschel, a Jewish woman. Immediately following the October 2023 Hamas attack on Israel, Heschel co-organized educational forums for students and faculty along with Tarek El-Ariss, the Arab chair of Middle Eastern studies (The Boston Globe, 2023). Their Arab–Jewish collaboration was widely praised for its ability to maintain nuanced dialogue and civility on campus when violence and polarization were poisoning numerous other schools.

Importantly, in all these examples of an updated leadership approach, expressing anger remains ever tricky for women. Anger must remain available for women to self-advocate, but they are warned to never "serve your anger hot" (Williams & Dempsey, 2014, p. 295); that is, it must always be tempered and exhibited with tight control. Though women have successfully taken on more historically masculine roles, feminine mandates and discriminating gender stereotypes most certainly remain (Rhode & Kellerman, 2007; Williams & Dempsey, 2014), and most women know it.

As a case in point, I am reminded of my three-year stint as the director of my psychoanalytic institute. Being the female leader at the helm had never been a personal goal, echoing the literature and likely reflecting my ongoing anxieties about self-promotion and ambition. I thus had no particular vision of leadership upon my arrival, and yet, as I evolved into the role, my style began to take shape. It incorporated both communal and agentic characteristics—mutuality, collaboration, and open-minded listening, blended with a voice of confidence, power, and self-assertion. Warmth with dominance, social with competence. This profile contrasted with that of prior male leaders of the institute, who were comfortable privileging power, independent problem solving, and restrained emotionality. With my more balanced approach to leadership, was I unconsciously trying to forestall anticipated envy and judgment from others, knowing the risks attendant to female leadership? No doubt. But, that said, the style I embodied allowed me to accomplish much during those three years and not repel too many others, as far as I knew. Getting along did remain a priority for me, though, one that neatly aligned with the stereotypical feminine role.

Looking back, my decision to accept this position of power was a significant growth-promoting experience that increased my comfort with aggression and enhanced my self-confidence. This result reinforces the ongoing need for women to summon the will to occupy visible seats of power for their own growth and for the confidence it inspires in others. At the end of my term, I felt particularly gratified when one of my colleagues evocatively captured her view of my leadership approach: "You succeeded in giving those you were working with a push and a hug all at the same time" (L. Fleischman, personal communication, June 18, 2016).

Additional behavioral strategies that have been useful to women on the rise include: (1) sitting at the table rather than the periphery; (2) speaking early and often in fewer, declarative sentences; (3) asserting one's opinion even when it is contrary; (4) resisting perfectionism, which inhibits risk taking (Phillips, 2015); (5) preventing idea theft by directing discussions back to one's own idea; (6) accruing support before meetings (Frankel, 2015; Phillips, 2015); (7) speaking publicly whenever possible and preparing for pushback (Phillips, 2015); (8) projecting confidence with voice, posture, and clothing and using humor as a "softener" (Williams & Dempsey, 2014)[12]; (9) including women of color and LGBT women in conversations (Williams & Dempsey, 2014); and (10) redefining power from "power-over" to "power to accomplish goals" (Feldt, 2014, p. 21).

Inspirationally, some have advocated for women to have the temerity and insight to escape from the male perspective's constricted views of female leaders and carve out their own vision of leadership, one free from cultural and self-imposed limitations (Reciniello, 2011). This, of course, is easier said than done, requiring steadfastness and resilience in the face of painful, patriarchal, and often distorting transferential reactions to one's leadership. But, as recent past president of the American Psychoanalytic Association Dr. Harriet Wolf notes, it is possible to get used to harsh perceptions of ourselves that can, in fact, help us be more confident about the reality of who we are and how we are seen: "I did connect with the courage that is part of the clinician in me . . . the courage to endure the anxieties and challenges of a deep dive with a patient—or with an organization" (Wolf, 2021, p. 146). In other words, being a psychoanalyst helps.

Notes

1 Wolf (2021) notes that men and women in psychoanalysis have been the exception regarding their greater openness to female leadership, notwithstanding the vilification and marginalization of others, such as Karen Horney.

2 D'Ercole (2023) points out that Clara Thompson was well aware of these lurking cultural and group impediments, and that her lack of arrogance and pattern of disguising her feelings were effective leadership tools that cunningly skirted objections from opponents and enhanced her ability to rise to the top of her field. This was in contrast to the more forceful, direct style of Karen Horney, which often posed problems for her.

3 Stacey Abrams, for example, has been credited as a self-advocate trailblazer; as a young Black girl growing up in Mississippi, she learned that if she did not speak up for herself no one else would (Leibovich, 2020).

4 Upon her appointment to the U.S. Supreme Court, Sandra Day O'Connor stated, "It made me very nervous. . . . It's all right to be the first to do something, but I didn't want to be the last woman on the Supreme Court. If I took the job and did a lousy job, it would take a long time to get another one" (Greenhouse, 2023).

5 There are numerous other patriarchal "givens" that are routinely perceived to be true but are in fact false, such as: (1) the male-hunter myth, which ignores the fact that, in most modern foraging societies, women have played a dominant role in bringing home the game, and attests to the persistent scholarly reluctance to acknowledge this reality (Miller, 2023); and (2) the myth that women are inherently worse at navigation than men, despite studies proving that it is childhood exposure to the physical world that shapes people's comfort and confidence in navigation, not their gender (Ro, 2024). Such gendered stereotypes are tenacious and consistently damaging to women.

6 There is actually a lower vocal sound that most people associate with authority and, correspondingly, people tend to prefer male and female leaders who have lower pitched voices (Bennett, 2019).

7 Some have found that, rather than reflecting a lack of assertiveness, women's tentative or "weak" language can be a useful strategy that softens their impact and thereby avoids activating those males who find female power threatening (Grant, 2023).

8 Conducted by Susan Madsen, leadership professor at Utah State University's business school.

9 Some claim that the lack of a central organizational structure in the Black Lives Matter movement has led to it compromising its goals and undermining its effectiveness, since leaderless groups tend to be directionless, unfocused, and unavoidably imbued with power dynamics that will always create a de facto leadership class (deBoer, 2023; Freeman, 1972).

10 These important advancements in our evolving view of leadership have incited predictable patriarchal backlash, as in the Trump presidency, White Christian nationalism, hypermasculinity, and misogynistic rulings such as the Dobbs case from an ultra-conservative U.S. Supreme Court. Such reactions are seen by many as efforts to restore power to those who feel they have lost it. Similarly, "as Black women have raised their profiles, they've raised right-wing hackles, making them targets of political aggression" (Blow, 2024).

11 Some caution, however, that invoking the notion of androgyny, as such, perpetuates damaging stereotypes about the differences between the sexes, since they are further internalized by women and men alike. "If certain traits or ways of thought remain 'womanly' and others 'manly,' familiar stereotypes about the differences between the sexes are perpetuated" (Keohane, 2007, p. 79).

12 Humor has been described in contrasting ways: as antifeminist and silencing (Billingsley, 2019), but also as a powerful and essential tool for female resistance, where women assert themselve's on their own terms to disrupt the male discourse— "silencing the ability of sexists to express their sexism" (Billingsley, 2019, p. 20).

Chapter 15

Reflecting on the Interviews

In this Chapter, I offer an overview of each of my six interviews, recapping each woman's unique path to power and the variables she sees as essential in her journey. I include a general description of each woman's relationship to her aggression (explored more extensively in Chapter 16) and point out when ideas from the women's leadership literature coincide with my interviewee's narrative, and when they diverge. Finally, I discuss some of the recurring themes that emerged across all the interviews.

Reflecting back upon my psychoanalytic conversations, not only did I learn richly from meeting these six impressive women, but, just as inspiring, they grew from our conversations as well. Many shared how they had come upon new insights even before our interviews began, often related to how they felt about the proposed undertaking and how they might approach it. Others let me know, as we spoke, that they were creating new hypotheses and reflections right then and there. These developments were enlivening and expansive for both of us.

As expected, these women had varying degrees of psychological mindedness, and my approach was to respect their stories, remain openly curious about them, and deepen them where possible. I reminded myself, as I now remind the reader, that my interviewees and I were not doing psychoanalysis (in contrast to Chapters 3 and 4, involving two psychoanalytic clinical vignettes). Where I might have pursued or challenged certain topics further in my clinical work, I refrained from doing so, respecting the nature of the interview format and aiming to maintain ongoing trust and safety for my interviewees.

Each of these conversations stands uniquely on its own. Each evolved spontaneously from an original set of questions about early home life, influences, setbacks, and successes, and expanded in its own direction. This progression

DOI: 10.4324/9781003476085-18

parallels the analytic process, as we continuously dream anew with each patient, find what is most alive, surprising, and growth-promoting (Ogden, 2021), and enthusiastically step into that space. The openness and flexibility of this approach kept these conversations fresh and unique, as individual perspectives on female power, aggression, ambition, and patriarchy emerged organically from each partnership. Each story paints a picture of female leadership, defined and redefined from within a particular personal history and cultural surround, underscoring the inherent value of the interview technique, notwithstanding its limitations in sample size and age similarities.[1]

Charlotte

Although Charlotte rose up to become the first female U.S. attorney in her state, a position of enormous authority and importance, her childhood dream was to take on the more socially acceptable role of a nurse. This, despite her pattern of always fainting at the sight of blood. Charlotte's early years were infused with the stimulating voices of male relatives who were highly successful attorneys and judges, although she noted that there was little actual attention given to her professional development, presumbably because she was a girl. "I certainly did not have a vision of being a lawyer."

As her talents were continually recognized through the years, Charlotte found her way to pursue her passion for the law and was able to reach impressive though unexpected heights. Once there, she was able to activate early models of vigorous self-assertion from both men and women in her family, which equipped her to view power as permissible, useful, and relationally safe: "It wasn't something to be shied away from; if you have it, use it, it's a tool in your toolbox." As well, her early exposure to constructive and modulated forms of anger helped her feel comfortable and unconflicted about mobilizing her own anger on the job: "When I got angry [at work], my voice would go up. I wasn't screaming, but I would be very clear about my expectations." Charlotte's ease and enjoyment in telling me her story were palpable, as she proudly conveyed the details of her creative and effective uses of aggression.

Charlotte revered and ultimately emulated her impressive male relatives, echoing the leadership literature's emphasis on the importance of paternal/male involvement in a girl's effort to self-potentiate. Her feelings were more ambivalent about her "difficult" mother, but, interestingly, our conversation sparked her new idea that it might actually have been her mother's "tartness" that helped her become a formidable litigator. She was thinking on the spot, infusing our conversation with vitality and fresh meaning. As a young girl, Charlotte was able to compensate for her mother's emotional harshness by comforting herself with her grandmother, who "was soft and plump and smelled like powder." She consistently found a way to obtain what she needed in the face of suboptimal circumstances or setbacks.

Charlotte internalized her family's mandate that males and females alike must keep their emotions inside, positive as well as negative ones. It was important to her that I understand that her family's taboo on emotional expression was imposed equally and not gender-based:

> Emotion was not the heart of my life . . . [it was] something to be fought back. . . . But I have to keep coming back to this governing principal: it wasn't my emotions as a female that was the problem; *nobody* showed emotion.

She learned early on to become self-sufficient and to bear strong feelings alone, given the family rule book, though she emphasized that her family's austere emotional style never compromised the love she felt from them.

As to the challenges faced by women leaders, Charlotte does not view the problem from a gendered perspective, which for her connotes a toxic victimhood.[2] "[You] can't wallow in what hasn't gone the way you wanted . . . or you'll be stuck in a never-ending spiral." Instead, as in the literature, Charlotte found creative ways to redefine power and ambition on her own terms, such as strategically and unapologetically using her femininity and appearance to enhance her effectiveness:

> I was born with certain attributes, and being female was one of them. . . . [If] it was going to help me, I didn't hesitate to use it, and [if] it might've been used against me, I didn't choose to buy into that.

When male colleagues commented on her appearance, rather than acting offended, Charlotte saw it as an opportunity, and volleyed back playfully, using "softeners," as described in the literature, to tone down her powerful image and delighting in the repartee. Her comfort with such interactions no doubt contributed to her overall effectiveness as she carried out her important position of authority.

Charlotte's town and its surround, which were literally founded by her ancestors, gave her a bedrock sense of stability and an invaluable cultural legacy (D'Ercole, 2023; Thompson, 1958) that she holds in the highest regard. It accented practicality, privacy, and understated humility. I witnessed the latter firsthand, when Charlotte consistently characterized her attributes and successes as merely "a collection of good luck and circumstances," downplaying the rather outstanding set of talents and personal attributes that undergirded her breakthrough leadership position.

Mia

Fierce, warm, and focused all at once, Mia is the president of a multi-billion-dollar foundation dedicated to improving health and human rights throughout the world. Hers is a role that lends itself to the updated, androgynous portrait of leadership described in the literature, one punctuated by stereotypically male strength that blends with a female relational style. I sensed these qualities immediately in Mia, when she complimented me early on in our interview and said she hoped she could be helpful.

In her role as leader, Mia focuses on building relationships and prioritizing her grantees over her own personal success. Her Asian immigrant background cemented an intense work ethic, such that she considers being pampered the sure road to ruin. As a result, she actively pursues personal discomfort and uncertainty, which she believes build critical tolerance for risk and failures: "What's preventing great female Korean doctors from being chairs of medical departments? . . . . stepping out of their comfort zones. That's one that I do. . . . To be a successful, high-achieving person, you must take risks."

Mia relished her annual summer visits to South Korea, where she enjoyed celebrity status. But her parents also emphasized humility and acculturation in America, embedding the family in a West Coast suburb with few Koreans, which minimized public awareness of her grandfather's international fame. Mia and I did not explore the details of why her parents chose to de-emphasize her family's prominence, though it did arouse my curiosity. Interestingly, the related issue of race was another infrequent topic in our interview, in contrast to its centrality in my interview with Margot (Chapter 11). It is not clear whether our lack of dialogue about race was an outgrowth of where Mia herself situates race psychologically, or whether other factors were at play, including my manner of addressing it between us.[3]

Mia's family surround included powerful, successful male and female figures she revered, particularly her father, who sacrificed a would-be easy life in South Korea for one that demanded a completely new start in America. Her mother had also worked in the nonprofit world and "could have had a great career in Korea but had to stop working and cater to my father." Mia's intense drive can be seen as a vindication of her mother's sacrificed dreams, as well as those of other Korean women with limited opportunities.

Like Charlotte, Mia emphasized the love she felt from her family, while also explaining that no one talked about feelings or was emotionally demonstrative. Anger could never be "served hot" (Williams & Dempsey, 2014), but rather had to be tightly controlled and minimized. Mia feels that possessing this skill benefits her today when navigating the "challenging personalities . . . and very demanding people" at her institution.

As to the patriarchy, Mia acknowledges, "Men still get away with saying and being a certain way, and women still get criticized on their appearance . . . so I say, brush your hair! We have to deal with it." She stressed that women should keep their eye on their goal and not take things personally or allow themselves to be sidetracked by insulting sexist behaviors.

For all her fierceness, in the end, Mia credits much of her success to a wonderful husband, echoing findings in the women's leadership literature, and insists that she is "not Type-A, not a killer, ambitious, or angry." Her way of understanding her own story of success, with its emphasis on the centrality of her husband's participation and minimization of her own ambition, struck me as an understandable effort to cope with a dominant culture that warns women not to be overly ambitious, angry, or strong— even when they evidently are.

Tess

Tess became a powerful academic leader, the first female dean of her law school, despite suffering early demons. One of my older interviewees, Tess grew up when female leadership was less visible, and the social training for girls was vastly different than it was for boys who, "from the beginning, know that they have to be something." Like other interviewees when they were young, Tess allowed herself only the socially acceptable dream of becoming Miss America, "the epitome for women."

Her early identifications were complicated by a successful and powerful father, intellectually oriented and curious, but explosive and inconsistently attentive as well. His intense drive to learn, epitomized by the dictionary that lived in the front seat of his car, captivated Tess, who credits him with her own curious mind and mirrors the importance of paternal involvement and encouragement noted in the women's leadership literature. But her father's rages and lack of reparative skills, culminating in his renunciation of his children, contaminated Tess's relationship to aggression, as did her mother's way of acting like a cold and silent "doormat" when she was angry, abandoning Tess in the process. Tess also shared that both her parents "were hitters," further exacerbating an already noxious situation. Unsurprisingly, she responded to this violent atmosphere by dissociating her aggression entirely. She could not acknowledge it in herself or in her family, no less mobilize it to her own advantage.

In addition, Tess's parents required her to regularly hide her achievements, part of their misguided effort to equalize the playing field between Tess and her less gifted sisters. This diminishment of Tess's talents sent her the toxic message that success will be envied by others and poison one's relationships if outwardly displayed (Harris, 2002). It caused Tess to shut down even further.

Aware from early on that her parents were troubled and preoccupied, Tess sought out local shopkeepers and her church as healthy alternatives for love and safety. "I just felt more loved by people on the outside." Her resiliency in the face of serious developmental threats (Masten, 2001) and her inherent potential toward growth (Winnicott, 1965) were manifold and inspiring.

As an adult, in her dean position, Tess continued to garner needed support and recognition from the few existing female deans across the country, as well as the female faculty in her law school, who thrilled at their first female leader. Her personal psychoanalytic work helped her reduce her reliance on such external validation by solidifying her confidence and her belief in her own self-worth. Her therapy was also integral when it came to her aggression, helping her retrieve what had once been dissociated due to developmental trauma, and marshal it for constructive use in her life. Tess's husband provided further opportunity to recharacterize her anger as a safe and essential part of self, encouraging her to express it with him and signaling that he was up to the task of tolerating it.

Despite hard and sustained therapeutic effort, however, Tess's ability to reliably access anger when needed can still be challenging, given its traumatic roots. At work, for example, she much preferred her role as dean to her prior role as associate dean, since the former accented cooperation and bridge building, but the latter required managing the "bombastic uncooperativeness" of faculty. This activated her own anger and drove her back into therapy. Similarly, in dealing with the patriarchy, Tess relies on the so-called feminine traits of humor and collaboration, rather than anger, to manage "the usual guy behavior," embodying a relationally oriented portrait of leadership and power, as described in the literature.

Tess's unique journey to success has been catalyzed by powerful psychoanalytic work that bridged positive aspects of her past—early recognition, curiosity, and ambition—with newly acquired tools to detoxify residual wounds, reclaim her once-owned aggression, and solidify a sturdy, more integrated sense of self. Tess's intense commitment to self-understanding and working through her early trauma in psychoanalysis made her a fascinating and inspirational interviewee.

Margot

Margot, the trauma surgeon who conducts complex emergency cases throughout the day and night, knows firsthand the "double jeopardy" of being female and Black in a patriarchal, racist system—one that requires her to prove her competence, excellence, and leadership over and over again, as well as bear the burden of representing her entire race in everything she does. She feels that the greater challenge for her is being female, though being Black is no easy ride, as she and I experienced firsthand in the enactment that saturated our earliest encounters (further detailed in Chapter 11).

Although I went about this project with much planning and care, my immediate racial enactment with Margot, omitting the subject of race from my pre-interview questions, contained a visceral taste of the solipsistic Whiteness (Holmes, 2021) and racism that she battles every day. Fortunately, our troubled encounter ushered in and prioritized the critical issue of race in our ensuing conversation, but not without my honest, pained admission to Margot about what I had done.

To recap, the trouble began when I realized our interview time was fast approaching and I had not yet received back the answers to my initial questions from Margot. As I paused to reflect upon what this might mean, I felt a jolt of shame as I realized I had failed to inquire about race and racism in any of my questions. I decided to approach Margot to try to correct the situation. With the arrival of these sobering thoughts, my shame began to shift and feel more tolerable as I thought through how to effect a repair.

This process occurred spontaneously and outside the realm of words (D. B. Stern, 2022), yielding a "new perception" (D. B. Stern, 2019, p. 17) of the troubling situation, and of Margot herself. I felt extremely grateful that she was ultimately willing to partner with me and accept an amended questionnaire that addressed her experiences of race and racism, personally and professionally. The breaching of our enactment yielded a loosening of the constrictions in our interpersonal field, allowing us to ultimately speak more freely and safely about her experiences (D. B. Stern, 2022), including those involving the challenges of racism.

As echoed in the leadership literature, Margot was able to cultivate a sturdy, effective voice at the family dinner table, in no small part due to her older sisters, who routinely chided her to "remind me I was nothing special." I bristled about whether she should have been better protected, but nonetheless could see that Margot believes she grew stronger from these affronts, refusing to allow shame to silence her and learning not to take slights too personally.

Margot's firm sense of self was further consolidated by her mother, an elementary school teacher, who understood and respected who she was despite their differences in temperament—Margot thoughtful and quiet, her mother bold and extroverted. In contrast, many a mother I have worked with clinically insisted on pushing her shy child to engage socially well before the child was comfortable, leaving chronic shame and resentment in the wake. Margot believes that her early maternal recognition enabled her to know and trust herself, as when she insisted on teaching before beginning medical school despite her father's fury at her decision. Margot knew she loved science and would eventually study medicine, and she was right. I imagine she was further motivated by her father's unrealized aspirations as well as his dreams for his daughter.

In their parenting style, Margot's mother and father effectively set aside gender stereotypes, which made way for Margot and all her sisters to pursue their dreams and succeed impressively in male-dominated fields. Such is the power of modeling that transcends ancient patriarchal dictates. I laughed out loud upon learning that Margot's mother told her teacher that no, Margot was not confused about gender; rather, her father was, in fact, the family cook and a beloved one at that. In the end, the teacher herself admitted that she wished her husband would also take over the family cooking. There was pride, self-confidence, and good humor in this family.

As for anger, Margot had permission in her family to notice aggression, though not "serve your anger hot" (Williams & Dempsey, 2014, p. 295). She knew well when her mother was angry by her tone and her look, not her raised voice. In parallel, the residents in Margot's operating room recognize her anger from her tone, pacing, and stance, not her volume. Margot's emotional control, learned in childhood, is critical to her success in an environment where she is perpetually at risk for being labeled the "bitch" and the "angry Black woman."

In her heavily male-dominated work world, Margot dresses her leadership in mostly male clothing—authoritative, solution-focused, and hyper-controlled. The surgeon in the operating room is the captain of the ship, ultimately liable for every action and event that occurs during an operation. Consequently, Margot must project rock-solid confidence, competence, and calm at all times. These mandates apply even more forcefully for a Black woman, though Margot may enjoy less pushback for her assertiveness than a White woman, due to the cultural stereotype of the "strong Black female." Margot embodies, in part, an updated style of leadership as described in the literature, one that privileges function and outcome over style; but, at the same time, maintains her image as the authority who cannot be "warm and cuddly."

Margot continues to push against her instincts as a natural introvert and heed the call to be a visible role model for younger Black female surgeons as well as the face of her hospital's diversity efforts—"the Black Tax," as she labels it. She has been told that her willingness to speak out about the challenges she has endured has been invaluable to Black residents, who have no other place to discuss the second-class citizenship they sometimes suffer.

When it comes to envy, Margot told me that she does experience it, particularly from other women, but she is unshaken. Instead, she channels her mother's commitment to hard work and positive results and focuses on seeing herself as so many others do, knowing deeply that "I am not just an average Joe."

Despite feeling like "an accidental leader," a pioneer status she never actively sought, Margot is able to acknowledge her aptitude for leadership though take pains to never flaunt it. Both her surprise at her stature and her humility about it are mirrored in the women's leadership literature and among all my interviewees. These qualities reflect (1) the cultural pressure on women to minimize success, (2) Margot's position as the first Black female across most situations, and (3) her family's limited emotional expressiveness. Instead, Margot maintains a quiet, abiding confidence in her abilities, never getting "puffed up" about any of it. "You get the recognition, or you don't, but you don't do it for that." Margot is a socially conscious, deeply thoughtful, and eminent female surgeon. She is a powerful role model for many and will undoubtedly remain so for years to come.

Sandra

As a U.S. magistrate judge, Sandra was the first female to hold a federal judicial office in her state. She won me over early on, as she explained that she had brainstormed with her family about my interview questions well before we met. And during our meeting, she let me know how engrossed she was in her storytelling despite fears of boring me. "I just know I'm totally engaged with the stories I'm telling you." It was immediately apparent to me that Sandra has a keen understanding of how to form a partnership.

As with other interviewees and reports in the leadership literature, Sandra dreamed smaller dreams in her early years, reflecting what was culturally most acceptable for women at the time. But, when the social upheaval of the nineteen sixties pried open the field of possibilities for professional women, Sandra's visions broadened, and she left teaching high school English for the more exciting chance to study law.

Sandra's dry humor delighted me when she quipped about "practicing aggression" early on by channeling Annie Oakley and Dale Evans with her long gun. She appreciated our subject matter and was comfortable enough in it to play, establishing an easygoing but serious atmosphere between us. Like others and the leadership literature, Sandra benefitted from early female models who were comfortable with their strength and gave implicit permission to work hard and achieve. As her beloved maternal grandmother taught her, you must get down on the floor, put your shoes on, make your bed, and get going. Every single day. As Sandra's primary caretaker, Nanny was all business, but also let her know she was special in many ways. She counseled that one must always have one's own income and independence, because any man you are with can up and die on you, even the good ones. It is thus no surprise that Sandra pictured herself growing up to be strong and independent-minded, and indeed became so. I knew it, too, from the way she never hesitated to improve upon my mirroring, capitalizing on its "off-ness" (Ogden, 2021) to more accurately express her own trusted and valued voice. Her deep belief in herself was inspiring.

Sandra's positive early modeling further congealed around her passion for her horses, which she fed, trained, and exercised regularly. She credits them with instilling in her a deep sense of responsibility, respect, and pride: "Those horses were essential in making me the person I am." Her participation in horse shows afforded a healthy view of competition and built up her tolerance for setbacks, both of which are often experienced as dangerous and challenging for young girls and women alike.

Like others I interviewed, Sandra cultivated a strong belief in her inherent value from her extended family, with whom she spent every evening as an only child. Yet here again was a family who was uncomfortable with outward demonstrations and declarations of affection, though Sandra never for a minute doubted how much they loved her and rejoiced in her success.

Unlike most other women I interviewed and those discussed in the leadership literature, Sandra had a distant and highly conflictual relationship with her father, who was unable to offer her the paternal recognition that others have consistently found so potentiating. He not only remarried a "wicked stepmother" after Sandra's mother died, but also betrayed Sandra by secretly bribing her daughter. Though so distant as to only refer to him by his first name, Sandra can nonetheless credit her father with caring for her sickly mother, reflecting her fair-mindedness and tolerance for complexity. Sandra's healthier family members and her own inner resilience have helped her cope with the wounds from her toxic paternal relationship.

Sandra's early experiences with hard work and strict self-control provided firm grounding for her future judgeships, where she always had to be even-tempered to command respect in her courtroom. She honed the skill of transforming her anger into something constructive, "being stubborn and sticking to the issues without being irate." While she could sometimes admittedly get "sort of nasty" when stressed, she reliably repaired the relational fallout with regular afternoon "cuppas," that made up for her bad behavior and provided a valued respite from a world where people's freedom often hangs in the balance. As seen in the literature, Sandra embodies an updated style of authority and power, where the so-called female qualities of collaboration and inclusivity combine with strength, emotional control, and focus on getting the job done.

Sandra's story about her misogynistic treatment at her judicial hearing, along with her awareness that her male counterparts regularly got away with being rude when she could not, demonstrate her keen awareness of the patriarchy and the tendency of men to dissociate their privilege and sexism (Tosone, 2009). But her credo has been not to avoid haranguing about it, since it is not going to move anyone forward, professionally or personally. Like Mia, who sees sexist behavior as the problem of the other, as well as Charlotte and Tess, who turn the misogynistic antics of male colleagues into something humorous, Sandra believes there are always ways to work through it.

Sandra's charming story about her travails learning to ride a bicycle is one of impressive and dogged perseverance. More challenged at bike riding than any kid she knew, the adult Sandra now rides ten miles a day no matter what. As she wisely observes, "if I don't learn from my setbacks, I'm in trouble." Even her discovery that she was not the smartest person in her law school class has been internalized as a valuable lesson that she can still make a difference, even when not the best.

Sandra is an impressive example of a woman who is comfortable dedicating her full self to her endeavors while staying humble in the process, as the patriarchy requires. "It's nice to have somebody listen to my story, and I'm honored and surprised you were given my name." She inspired me with her commitment to self-improvement, her willingness to face each day with rigorous determination, and, all the while, her ability to appreciate the humorous, light side of life.

Shirley

From the earliest way she described herself, I had a good sense of the force with which Shirley, the chief technology officer at a renowned biomedical research institute, meets life. That is, with unbridled curiosity, energy, and drive to expand. "I'm kind of a scavenger . . . I learn from and take whatever I can get." The vivid scrappiness of her imagery captured the intensity with which Shirley devours information wherever she finds herself, fearless about incorporating new perspectives and embracing change. Demonstrating that what gets talked about gets lived out (Levenson, 1983, 1996), Shirley told me that, when it was hard for her to answer my initial questionnaire about her early role models, she arrived at the epiphany that her early life feels uncomfortably delinked from her current one. Originally, she lived for the theater and piano in Israel. Today, she is a research scientist and technology officer in the United States, recognized for her superior productivity. Though Shirley's two distinct lives may feel segregated in important ways, she nonetheless told me, "The older I get, the more I realize that my formative years in Israel have 100 percent influenced my take on life . . . both the time and place . . . and my own personal family background."

Shirley credits Israel with fostering her strong sense of humility, because you are judged on objective rather than subjective standards. "If you're not the best at everything, it's okay." She is impatient with American education, where students like her daughter are rewarded for everything they do and easily develop an unrealistic view of themselves as a result. As with other interviewees, Shirley feels that her childhood surround anchored her and instilled in her the value of hard work, perseverance, and resilience. Making things too easy, as all my interviewees noted, compromises one's grit and motivation.

When describing her parents, Shirley movingly explained that their background as Holocaust survivors permeated the culture at home, teaching her to take nothing for granted and to focus only on significant problems, rather than minor inconveniences. I was touched as she shared that going through these early memories with me was "really quite special" for her. The stability of home and family no doubt undergirds Shirley's deep belief in her inherent value, her emotional regulation, and her outstanding leadership.

Shirley is a standout leader whose capacity for goal-directed intensity, combined with expressiveness, warmth, and insight, have consistently advanced her in her professional life. Pursuing her doctorate in microbiology led to heading her laboratory, which led to her overseeing her entire research institute, even though she was not the one actually pursuing these advancements. Fair-minded and reasonable, Shirley believes the most important goal is getting the job done to the highest standard. She projects total transparency and clear expectations, modeling that the job is just a job; it is not personal. As with all my other interviewees, Shirley stresses the importance of not overly personalizing interactions, which builds tolerance for setbacks, maintains perspective, and models that "who I am is different than what I can accomplish" (Reynolds, 2015, p. 101). But she finds that the women she works with often have difficulty in this area. They compromise their forward motion by becoming overly invested in professional positions they have worked for years to attain, and struggling to accept feedback, which can feel like an indictment of one's overall self.

Shirley's view of the patriarchy is remarkably consistent with other interviewees. As she observes, "The world isn't becoming equal anytime soon, and women need to learn how to interact." She advises that women should avoid coming to the table as victims and compensating by being overly aggressive. She believes that male mentorship, with its hyperfocus on results and efficiency, can help women relate more effectively in a patriarchal world.

Shirley projects an updated female leadership style that is emotionally controlled, collaborative, focused on the overall good, and non-hierarchical, as learned in the Israeli military. But, similar to Margot the surgeon, Shirley incorporates a male-oriented approach in her leadership that is direct, efficient, and pragmatic in order to thrive in her male-dominated scientific world. I imagine that her Israeli background, with its typical emphasis on straightforwardness and frankness, further reinforces her chosen style of leadership.

At the end of our conversation, in spite of all her moxie and grit, Shirley surprised me by dramatically shifting self-states: "It's weird for me to have a conversation where I'm doing 100 percent of the talking. I'd love to set up a time to hear your story." The normative unconscious is alive and well in even the most successful women.

Recurring Themes

Standing back from these unique and illuminating interviews, what can we say we have learned from this effort? Certainly, that each woman's perspective on power and leadership style will amalgamate her individual history, character, race, and culture. As well, each woman's approach will incorporate the politics of the moment and the particular context at hand—the regimented operating room, for example, will call for a different type of leader than the large nonprofit or technology company. Further, each woman's version of aggression will be continually reimagined and reinvented over the course of her lifetime as it unfolds. Given the ever-shifting variables that recursively influence the female leader, there is ultimately "no single answer to how to succeed as a woman in a professional world" (Williams & Dempsey, 2014, p. 15), certainly no right or wrong way to do it. Each woman must thus call upon her own creativity, ingenuity, and grit to find ways of flipping the liability of being female into an asset, transforming disempowering female symbols such as nastiness into resources that catalyze energy and growth (Lorde, 1981; Zuckerman, 2019). Gender is an infinitely complex part of identity, and we must each decide what it means to us (Williams & Dempsey, 2014) and how to embody it. Each profile of female leadership will be decidedly different.

But, alongside the unique portrait that will always characterize each female leader, we can also notice several commonalities that existed across all six narratives in this book. That is, there were certain features that all my interviewees named as critical to their success, which I will now review.

Chief among these recurring variables was the presence of loved ones who believed in the inherent value, abilities, and potential of the women.

These critical figures provided the encouragement to achieve and take risks, and modeled regulated forms of emotions that provided the building blocks for constructive uses of aggression and power. In so doing, these essential figures bypassed gender stereotypes, either directly or implicitly, ultimately affording permission for each woman to realize her dreams and ambitions and execute them with determination, enthusiasm, and pride. Tess, who lacked such authorizing people in her immediate family, bravely sought them out in her church, with local purveyors, and in a life-changing psychoanalysis. These substitutes enabled Tess to develop the missing confidence and inspiration she needed to mobilize her notable talents and achieve success.

We can also see, across the full spectrum of the interviews, the well-developed capacity for emotional regulation and resilience, as these women coped one by one with life's challenges, including a "miserable" freshman semester at college; a new American culture; an explosive father; racism, a deceitful father; and a critical, depressed mother. This observed control and determination included continually deciphering how to outwit the patriarchy, a reality that was uniformly acknowledged but typically dealt with by "letting it pass." These women firmly believed that their success constituted the most potent revenge against patriarchal inequities, and that responding with emotional reactivity or female victimhood endangered that result. Instead, they regularly employed humor to de-escalate sexist slights and practiced not personalizing feedback, which they knew could jeopardize their forward movement. But, in addition to the critical emotional control that undergirded all these constructive ways of being, each woman also described an early home environment that lacked ongoing discussions about feelings and outward displays of affection. This was a curious and surprising finding that I delve into more deeply in Chapter 16.

Finally, for all these women, their path toward success was neither straightforward nor even imagined early on. Their early visions for their futures were notably modest, but gradually shifted toward grander scales as their talents and skills were continually recognized and actualized. Their paths toward power and influence were thus circuitous but ascendent, as they leveraged positive opportunities and internalized mentors who believed they were capable of more than they themselves thought possible (Van der Kolk, 2014). Though most of the women were surprised by where they ultimately landed, once there, they came to fully believe that they had what it took to succeed. This was a deeply inspiring finale to their stories. That said, these women were also uniformly modest and private about their success. Remarkably, all six shared with me how awkward they felt talking only about themselves during our time together, how special it was to have the chance to tell me their story, and, for some, even their surprise that they were among those selected to do so.

In sum, the recurring themes that appeared in the narratives of all six women as they reflected upon their success included: (1) the affirming presence of loved ones who fostered their deep belief and quiet confidence in themselves; (2) the capacity to emotionally regulate and transform raw aggression into usable forms for resilience and growth; (3) a success trajectory that began as modest but reached increasingly greater heights as mentors were internalized and opportunities for growth were capitalized; and (4) the deep belief that they were well-suited to their influential positions, although remaining humble about their success was also felt to be essential.

Notes

1 Given patriarchal constraints and typically indirect career paths, women often reach leadership positions only when they are older, as with most of my interviewees.
2 The notion of "victim feminism" is often applied in a political context, which I chose not to pursue with Charlotte.
3 Some have noted that, while all political topics will intersect with issues of race, and it is an essential lens through which to understand the world, it is not the only one (deBoer, 2023).

Chapter 16

A Closer Look at Two Recurring Themes

Navigating the Patriarchy and the Impact of the Early Emotional Environment

I will now delve more deeply into two specific subjects raised by my interviewees, as they are important enough to merit further discussion and reflection. They include (1) each woman's chosen ways of navigating the patriarchy and the potential implications of these choices, and (2) the early emotional environment of each woman's home, including its impact on their developing emotional regulation and use of aggression.

Navigating the Patriarchy and Cultural Implications

The question of how we as a culture, regardless of gender, can most successfully address the patriarchy is a critical one. Among my interviewees, each woman's road to success necessitated creative and adaptive pathways to navigate this widely recognized danger zone. And, in each case, the interviewee candidly acknowledged the existence and intractability of patriarchal inequities, but chose not to directly call them out, guided by the firm belief that success achieved was the best revenge against sexism, and that reactivity or victimhood could compromise it. Instead, the women practiced not personalizing negative feedback and employing humor to de-escalate sexist slights that came their way.

Recall Mia, whose feedback to her colleague who had been the target of a racist, sexist slight was that she was allowing the man's ugly remarks to misdirect her focus and hamstring her career path—"Why would you do that?" Mia asked, compellingly. "He doesn't even matter to you." As well, Charlotte and Tess told me they regularly witnessed patriarchal behaviors in the lawyers with whom they worked, but they routinely reached for humor and playfulness to de-escalate sexist slights, rather than further empowering them with direct regard. "You look fabulous—that tie!" quipped Charlotte. She actually recoiled at even conceptualizing such interactions in

DOI: 10.4324/9781003476085-19

gendered terms, since she believes this connotes a problematic victimhood and does not in any way further her goals. Sandra was presented with blatant and toxic discrimination at her nomination hearing, but she defanged it impressively by regulating her internal fury and shrewdly outfoxing the judicial bully who tried to block her appointment. Considering this range of responses to patriarchal insults and firebombs, it is important to ask: what do we make of these methods of disarming them?

As for humor, we must wonder whether using it to foil sexism is problematic, even though it may strategically stop the action for the moment. Humor can be understood from several different perspectives. It can be seen as a defensive maneuver that leaves sexism problematically unaddressed, and women safely shielded from distasteful direct conflict; an avoidance, if you will. From another perspective, however, humor can be seen as a form of creative aggression that cleverly sidesteps sexist affronts, neutralizes their threat, and lays bare what they really are, for all to see. "Well, don't *you* look nice today!" Charlotte jauntily retorts. When landing well, humor presents the image of a woman who is confident and undeterred by male attempts to take her down. She is able to proceed uninterrupted toward her goal and, in the process, disrupts male efforts to silence and intimidate her. "The physical act of laughter is the ultimate tool of playful protest . . . a striking tool of resistance . . . an inroad toward social justice (Chess, 2021, paras 1–4). Simply said, humor works.

As a recent example, while participating in the 2024 Republican Party presidential debates, Nikki Haley made headlines with her clever response to a competitor's gendered attack on her stiletto heels. Rather than a fashion statement, Haley quipped, she considers her heels a source of ammunition. Her humorous and creatively aggressive response succeeded in reminding the public about the ongoing double standard for powerful women; at the same time, it portrayed her skillfulness in taking it on. As seen with others, Haley strategically took the most feminine of objects, the high heel, and transformed it into a weapon of power that successfully muted a gendered attack (Bennett, 2023).

In one sense, the women of the twenty-first century have the privilege of pursuing their ambitions without having to take direct aim at the patriarchy. They are the beneficiaries of feminist ancestors, from ancient times to the present, who fought the hard fight to gain equal rights for women—the rights to vote, access education, receive more equitable pay, control their own bodies (although this remains under constant assault), and more.

Standing on the shoulders of giants such as Susan B. Anthony, Betty Friedan, Simone de Beauvoir, Nancy Pelosi, and Ruth Bader Ginsburg to name the barest few, today's woman can trust that her historical subjugation has been sufficiently marked and incorporated into the cultural discourse, that she needn't call it out directly as she advances herself. It is arguable that the established unacceptability of sexism and harassment, at least in American culture, allows for the use of more subtle coping strategies, such as humor, deflection, containment, and collaboration, to stanch them.

Nonetheless, does this kind of accommodation, the choice to let it pass, compromise women's overall thrust toward greater equality by failing to directly call out sexism and attacks on powerful women? Should Hillary Clinton have dared to be more directly aggressive toward Donald Trump when he stalked her in the infamous 2016 U.S. presidential debate, rather than maintaining epic self-control? Clinton understood well her double bind in that moment and the steel trap of reacting more forcefully. I would argue, that in light of the stubborn reality of such patent sexism, the use of humor by my interviewees and other female leaders is justified, as it artfully clears the path for them to rise. We know that the importance of women joining the social discourse and representing female vantage points cannot be over-emphasized. When Ruth Bader Ginsburg joined her on the U.S. Supreme Court, Sandra Day O'Connor remarked, "I can't tell you how happy I was when she got to the court. It makes a night and day difference to have women on the bench" (Greenhouse, 2023, p. 150). Further, when female politicians and C-suite executives occupy visible seats of power, they represent iron-clad proof of the possibility, acceptability, and effectiveness of women in such positions. John Roberts, chief justice of the court, crisply captured this essence upon the death of Sandra Day O'Connor. "Her leadership shaped the legal profession, making it obvious that judges are both women and men" (VanSickle, 2023).

Call it out directly, or let it pass; there is certainly no easy or simple answer to this central question. However, as previously proposed, I believe that addressing patriarchal behaviors in a way that minimizes the alienation of women, male colleagues, and authority figures alike is an effective mindset that furthers the overriding goal of propelling women to powerful and visible positions—at least in the present cultural moment. Leading with victimhood, despite its unfortunate accuracy, risks feeding patriarchal stereotypes that women are whiny, weak, and not resilient, as Charlotte the U.S. attorney warned. And as Sandra the U.S. magistrate judge observed:

"If you are always haranguing about it, it's not going to move you forward, professionally or personally. There are ways to work through it."

Alongside such optimism, however, liberating oneself from patriarchal constrictions remains complex and fraught today. Women are still compelled to work creatively within forces that consciously and unconsciously tarnish perceptions of the female voice, a voice that is still too often heard as strident, masculine, too loud, or whiny. As such, women are called upon to creatively reverse symbols of female disempowerment and reposition them to their advantage—Thatcher's handbag, Pelosi's pearls, Clinton's nastiness, Haley's stilettos, or Beyoncé's bitchiness, which she recently reinforced: "Eventually, they realize this bitch will not give up" (Buchanan, 2023, para. 9). This important goal must also be accompanied by the hard work of leaving a forceful impact that attests to women's effectiveness, notwithstanding their need to work harder than male colleagues and tolerate judgment and condescension along the way.

Asking women to step up and occupy positions of leadership does not come easily, given the widely known relational dangers of self-assertion and expressed aggression. It requires raw courage to push forward despite the discouragement and pushback that awaits. But "focused with precision it [anger] can become a powerful source of energy, serving progress and change . . . a radical alteration in those assumptions underlying our lives" (Lorde, 1981, para. 17).

Early Emotional Environment: Positive and Negative Implications

Each of my interviewees described the emotional climate in her home as one that lacked a focus on (1) naming, articulating, and expressing feelings; (2) being listened to from an emotional perspective; and (3) having one's internal experience understood. And, in some cases, families actively discouraged such ways of being. As Charlotte reported: "Emotion was not the heart of my life . . . that was something you just didn't do." This finding leaves us with much to ponder.

First and foremost, my sample size of only six women represents a group of women whose lives happened to work out impressively, notwithstanding their early emotional climates. In fairness, these stories cannot be relied upon with any confidence to assess how an emotionally limited environment will affect development, or how it might help young girls potentiate themselves. Further, it is possible, even likely, that those interviewed are constitutionally more resilient and capable of locating and leveraging the recognition needed to fully launch themselves despite its limited availability at home.

Nonetheless, it is still important to ponder the effects of an early environment that de-emphasizes emotions and emotional expression, since the fundamental ideals and constructs of our profession assert that doing so—recognizing and naming feelings and finding ways to appropriately speak out about them—builds healthy, sustaining relationships with self and others over a lifetime. "For all of us, because we are practitioners of the talking cure, verbal reflection will always hold a special and honored place in our clinical theory and practice" (D. B. Stern, 2019, p. 21). I will thus take some time to explore the issue of a purportedly limited early emotional environment in its most positive light and thereafter consider its possible pitfalls.

From the positive end, the explicit and ongoing verbal discussion of feeling states may not always be necessary to successfully communicate to children that they are loved and valued, and that their perspectives are sound and impactful. As one interviewee noted, "I knew my family loved me because of the way they looked at me and smiled and were interested and spent time with me." Another shared: "They weren't demonstrative, but they were always proud when I did well in school or in anything and told me I was special in many ways." These positive responses prompt us to ask how much words themselves matter when love and recognition are experienced as otherwise present and presumably communicated nonverbally, as in these six stories.

Relatedly, the analytic literature reminds us that verbal language is only one kind of symbolic system among many, and that the most important clinical events actually unfold outside the realm of verbal language (D. B. Stern, 2019, 2023). Further, the relationship between the verbal and nonverbal has been one of the more perplexing problems in psychoanalysis, both historically and currently:

More recently, the nonverbal has become at least equally important in many psychoanalytic theories and accounts; and in some contemporary accounts of treatment, especially those contributed by Daniel Stern (1985) and the Boston Change Process Study Group (2010), the nonverbal has, actually overtaken and surpassed the verbal. The verbal, meanwhile, has not lacked for recent defenders of its own (e.g., Harris, 2014; Kirshner,

2014; Litowitz, 2011, 2014; Loewald, 2000; Ogden, 1997, 1998, 1999, 2016; Spivak, 2014; Vivona, 2003, 2006, 2009a, 2012, 2013, 2014).

(D. B. Stern, 2023, p. 20)

Stern (2019, 2023) concludes that, in reality, both the verbal and the nonverbal realms unite under the broad construct of language, and the most important distinguishing factor is not verbal or nonverbal, but rather whether language is meaningful; that is, whether it contributes to "the construction of spontaneous, creative living" (D. B. Stern, 2019, p. 21).

But as to early emotional development, parents are not always aware of when their behaviors are experienced by their children as meaningful and contributive to their "spontaneous, creative living." As an example, I recall my surprise when one of my children mentioned how personally meaningful it was to him when he was young that I always ended any phone call I was on when he entered the room. He felt that my actions enabled me to focus more fully on him. Such a small piece of wordless behavior was in fact noticed and made a positive difference to my son. It signaled that he was a priority and mattered enough for me to always end my call.

Feelings, as such, are regularly communicated wordlessly from parents to children all the time, and as psychoanalytic elders (Levenson, 1984; Sullivan, 1953) have taught, children are great interpreters of their parents' nonverbal behavior, anxiety and pleasure alike. Charlotte, for example, intuited her inherent value from her inclusion in her relatives' discussions about their legal cases. Even Tess felt uplifted early on, when her father vigorously competed with her and challenged her to strive in school. Margot also knew that her father expected her to attend medical school, implicitly communicating that she had the talent to make that happen. Words were not there, but the message of value and worthiness was powerfully communicated nonetheless.

We also know that parents can sometimes overdo it when it comes to noticing and initiating discussions about their children's emotions. There are many unfortunate stories about the children of therapists who experienced a laser focus on their emotions that felt intrusive and annoying. These children resented the ever-hovering curiosity about their inner states and sometimes reacted by shutting down completely. As clinicians, we also know that words can be defensively used to cover up authentic feelings, as when a patient's flood of words diverts conversation away from more essential matters like the therapeutic relationship. From the opposite direction, silence can be a powerful communicator, both positively and negatively. Suffice it to say, words are only one method by which we powerfully communicate meaning to one another.

Alternatively, an optimal balance can be sought between noticing and naming a child's feelings while, at the same time, respecting her privacy and right to work out internal and external conflicts on her own. This approach preserves the joy, satisfaction, and confidence inherent in doing so, and furthers a child's faith that she can manage life with competence, having had the chance to experiment, fail, and persevere along the way. From this vantage point, privileging the verbal expression of emotions in parenting children may be somewhat overrated, and actions may well speak louder than words.

Another source of positive esteem and motivation that may have accrued in my interviewees' families without the direct use of words was an emphasis on ambition and achievement. This likely carried an implicit statement of worthiness and the privileging of self-assertion and self-actualization over the patriarchal pressure to marry and caretake. This perspective is reminiscent of the cross-cultural research on high-achieving women who uniformly reported that their fathers' encouragement to achieve, rather than their emphasis on marrying, undergirded their drive toward success and power.

In the end, Charlotte, Mia, Margot, Sandra, and Shirley each shared their unwavering conviction that they felt loved and valued by their families, that their parents and elders believed in them, and were uplifted by their successes. Their descriptions of steady, meaningful emotional support early on was perceived as essential to their impressive journeys, as Charlotte emulated her father and grandfathers' legal acumen, Mia dutifully embodied her immigrant family's intense drive to succeed, Margot became a doctor to fulfill her father's dreams, Sandra pushed ahead day after day as her beloved grandmother taught, and Shirley strove to be her very best, motivated by an early culture that valued meritocracy over all. And for Tess, whose parents were too self-absorbed to attend to her with any regularity, she mobilized around the deep support she received from others in her community, adjusting her shaky self-image to better align with their appreciation of her.

All in all, we can comfortably assert that these successful women may not have had families that directly discussed feelings, but that deep belief in their worthiness and ability was nonetheless powerfully communicated in myriad ways that bypassed the use of explicit words.

Now, as promised, I would like to consider the possible ways that the quality of the emotional environments in question might also have had a downside. That is, despite the positive modeling of emotional regulation and active support for emerging ambition, whether a home environment lacking attunement and space for processing emotions might also leave behind a negative imprint, since "Key experiences with significant others become internalized and then play a central role in determining each of our unique personalities and the way we engage and even shape our current world" (Hirsch, 2011, p. 2).

As clinicians, we know much about the dangers of burying strong feelings over time and the toxic buildup of silence and resentment that occurs when so much feeling is layered over and unprocessed. Intense feeling states do not just go away despite one's best efforts and wishes that it were so. As well, we know that the ability of children and adults alike to transform aggression into constructive and usable forms relies upon experiences of feeling understood and being seen by the other (Coates, 1998; Knox, 2013; Pizer, 2003; Reckling & Buirski, 1996). In other words, when we feel understood and accepted, the emotional safety and recognition provided helps us succeed in taming our emotions and converting aggression into useful forms. Did my interviewees experience this kind of emotional attunement in their early development from their parents or other significant figures? Not so for Tess, whose misattuned early environment left her ill-equipped to work through the aggression she experienced from her elders and within herself. If parents cannot provide this recognizing function for a child, she is left with only raw forms of aggression that can poison her view of herself and her relationships. I will look more closely at this issue later in this chapter by investigating the interviewees' home environments and their early experiences as they relate to aggression.

Another question that arises concerning the early emotional environments of my interviewees relates to the focus on ambition and achievement. Might such an emphasis, without concurring attention to how that is experienced, result in a child who strives impressively but does so primarily for the purpose of legitimizing herself in her parents' eyes and her own? In this sense, the child's achievement may represent a defensive adaptation to an environment that lacked sufficient recognition and mirroring of her overall value. Given the interview format we cannot be sure, but the question remains important to ponder.

Finally, I wonder whether the early emotional environments of my interviewees left a negative trace on their relationships over a lifetime, knowing that one can have professional success but still suffer intimate relationships that are bleak and distant (Van der Kolk, 2014). For example, might it be difficult to process relational aggression—competition, anger, envy—between friends, partners, or colleagues, since processing relational ruptures and movement to repair were neither practiced at home nor otherwise encouraged in the homes of the interviewees? This important question is also difficult to fully address, since the majority of my interviewees (other than Tess, who weighed in heavily on the toxic effects of her family's rage) were resolute that their nuclear families were entirely loving and supportive, rendering the question of later relational fallout challenging to explore. In addition, given limited time together, the primary focus of my interviews was how the patriarchy and aggression were managed professionally, the central theme of this book.

With that said, we can home in on how the early environments in question affected the women's ability to acknowledge and regulate emotions and aggression, since that information was more readily accessible in our conversations.

Early Emotional Environment and its Impact on Emotional Regulation and Use of Aggression in the Interviewees

Having established that emotionally reserved environments can still effectively communicate deep recognition and support to children, we can now wonder about how these climates affect a child's developing emotional regulation and use of aggression. I have carved out these two interconnected variables for further analysis, since they were consistently cited by all my interviewees as critical to their success. That is, all six women believed that their ability to remain outwardly calm when waters got rocky and creatively apply their aggression provided the bedrock for their ascension. But how did they master these life skills if feelings were rarely, if ever, discussed in their families, and emotional regulation was not actively practiced? In other words, if "feeling listened to and understood changes our physiology" (Van der Kolk, 2014, p. 234) and is the "wellspring of physiological self-regulation" (Van der Kolk, 2014, p. 213), how were these vital functions actualized in an emotionally limited environment? I will explore this complex question through the specific lens of each interviewee's unique family configuration.

Charlotte told me that it was almost shameful in her family to dwell on her feelings of sadness or self-pity when something upset her. Instead, she was instructed to "just not think about it . . . your emotions are just something to be fought back." The emotional rules of this family were so strictly laid down that when Charlotte's paternal grandfather died, her father developed alopecia overnight "because of his inability to express grief." As Charlotte herself said: "That sort of speaks volumes about how we were . . . you just didn't talk about things . . . so I learned to control that." Did the lack of a space to discuss emotions affect Charlotte's ability to regulate them? And what eventually happened to those emotions if they had to be processed alone and were explicitly devalued? Charlotte did make mention of sometimes being upset, but she also added, "I don't remember being angry. . . . I'd be disappointed when things wouldn't go my way, but I would process through it. I don't remember screaming or yelling." Did Charlotte pay a price for having to manage her emotions all on her own?

As it happens, more significant information emerged as Charlotte and I continued talking, and another feature of her early life shed meaningful light on this subject. Almost parenthetically, Charlotte gently told me about her maternal grandmother, who was "soft and plump and smelled like powder . . . the softest person in my life, who I turned to when I think of emotions." So, as it turns out, there was someone in Charlotte's life who represented an emotional refuge when things got tough, even though her feelings were not otherwise attended to. The soft and plump grandma who smelled like powder offered Charlotte, at least symbolically, a shoulder to lean on when she was hurting and a key figure whose compassion and recognition argu-ably provided the building blocks for Charlotte's internal emotional control.

As to power and aggression, Charlotte was also fortunate that acting in a regulated though forceful and powerful way, like the prominent lawyers and politicians in her family, was both permitted and highly valued. Identifying with these larger-than-life male figures allowed her to grow up relatively unconflicted about power (relatively, since the normative unconscious is always a competing factor), and to exercise it in a controlled, unapologetic way to actualize her goals. With all this in mind, we can propose that Charlotte benefitted from effective models of emotional control and constructive forms of aggression, despite what at first glance appeared to be a more emotionally constrained environment.

Mia's early emotional environment, as it relates to her emotional reg-ulation and experience of anger and aggression, was, like Charlotte's, complicated. She felt loved by her parents and extended family, but she also described them as not emotionally demonstrative or expressive. Nonetheless, Mia grew up with great confidence in herself and the ability to live with "discomfort, change, and a lot of ambiguity." How is this so? As it turns out, Mia was highly influenced by a dominant family narrative that starred her father, who rejected his pampered life in South Korea and courageously reinvented himself in America without his cloak of privilege. His and the family's emphasis on containing emotions enough to push beyond one's comfort and welcome mistakes along the way was internalized by Mia and further solidified as the middle child who had to work hard to achieve. Mia lives out this credo with intense dedication in her prominent professional role.

When it comes to aggression, Mia's story is similarly complex. She describes herself as "always having combat boots on" to redress gender discrimination in South Korea, as well as her mother's traditional role of supporting her family but sacrificing her own dreams. Given this vivid description, I thought I had a good sense of Mia's relationship to anger and aggression, but she took me by surprise when she later said: "Anger is something I have not had to deal with personally as much myself. . . . I wasn't Type A, not a killer, ambitious or had anger." Alternatively, Mia thinks of herself as a skillful tactician, much like her paternal grandfather, who never resorted to yelling and was a "masterful negotiator." Curiously, Mia does not think of her deft negotiating skills as deriving from her aggression and ambition, but rather in opposition to them—she feels she is not Type A, ambitious, or angry.

My own assumption is that Mia's need to know herself in this way is grounded in the patriarchal pressure for women to be relationally oriented, collaborative, and non-aggressive, rather than antagonistic, confrontational, and angry. Her palpable discomfort in thinking of herself as aggressive is also likely related to her one-sided view of aggression's more destructive features, a common misconception particularly when describing women. This is precisely why I emphasize the importance of repositioning aggression (see Chapter 2) so that it includes the most alive, vital, and constructive human elements in addition to the more malignant ones (Harris, 1997, 2002). My take on Mia's understanding of aggression was further evidenced when she happened to mention in passing that she was not entirely clear about the meaning of the phrase "nasty women." Her confusion is shared by many.

Tess was the only woman among the six interviewed who held a more consciously conflicted view of her parents and her home environment, going as far as to say that, although she felt loved, she experienced far more affirmation and support from those outside her home. When it came to her ability to emotionally regulate and live comfortably with her anger and aggression, Tess's home offered no model; rather, it was a source of great anxiety, confusion, and fear. Her father was an emotionally damaged authoritarian who was regularly out of control, and her mother was cold, passive, and isolative. When fury erupted in this household, neither of Tess's parents had the ability to acknowledge or repair the ensuing damage, which left Tess and her sisters in states of chronic confusion and fear. So much so that Tess's psychic solution to the disquietude was to completely dissociate her own aggression.

Furthering her difficulties with aggression, Tess's parents made a point of regularly tamping down her academic accomplishments and successes, which sent the message that ambition and success are relational killers and must therefore be kept hidden. It has only been through her rigorous and sustained psychoanalytic work and an insightful, accepting husband that Tess has felt safe enough to acknowledge her own aggressive parts and strivings, to empower them in her life, and to allow her successes to be seen and known. Defying her expectations, the important people in her life have routinely applauded her when she has dared to do so.

Margot's family is also remembered as lacking the direct expression of parental love and recognition, even self-labeling: "We're the S. family, we don't have feelings." How did this sterile emotional environment impact Margot's development of affect regulation and her relationship to aggression? Margot's home offers a good example of one that succeeds in communicating growth-promoting affirmation and mirroring, the building blocks of self-control and creative aggression, without relying specifically on words to do so. Her mother was deeply attuned and supportive from Margot's earliest years, implicitly communicating her awareness and acceptance of Margot's temperament and preferences. In addition, there was never yelling or a loss of emotional control in Margot's home, although her parents' avoidance of outright anger may also reflect their effort to skirt racist and sexist tropes about excess anger in Black women and Black people.

The taboo on outright anger in her home did not mean that Margot was unaware when her mother was experiencing it. As children do (Sullivan, 1953), Margot anticipated and intuited her mother's anger through the tone of her voice and the seriousness she embodied. Margot internalized this style of regulating herself and managing her aggression and calls upon it routinely in the operating room, where emergent situations require her authority to be respected and unquestionably obeyed by those with whom she works.

Although Margot's father had much difficulty acknowledging and expressing his anger, a likely consequence of his early parental abuse, this was countered by Margot's mother's comfort with her aggression. Additionally, both parents' ability to bypass traditional gender norms enabled Margot's positive use of aggression despite her father's limitations.

Managing emotions and aggression has proved essential to Margot in executing her professional role and navigating racist and sexist challenges in her path. "As a Black woman, I cannot be publicly angry . . . or even emotional. . . . If I did what male colleagues do in these situations, I would be the bitch." As her interviewer, I had the benefit of directly experiencing Margot's constructive management of her aggression, when she steadily and graciously allowed me to amend my pre-interview questions to ensure that they addressed critical issues about race.

Sandra was yet another interviewee who described her early home as not emotionally demonstrative or featuring a lot of "I love you's." Despite this lack of outward demonstrations of affection, however, Sandra was as sure as Annie Oakley that she was loved by her parents and extended family. She felt they reliably showed pleasure in response to her achievements and told her she was special in many ways. Her resulting inner confidence and comfort with emotions were immediately evident in our interview, as in her quip that she must have enjoyed her aggression even as a child, given her regular target practice. Unthreatened by aggression, Sandra was able to acknowledge and be playful about it during our conversation. Her comfort level in this respect was effective in creating a wide open field for us to discuss how harnessing aggression has been pivotal in her life.

Sandra credits her early comfort with managing emotions to her work with horses, which she fed, exercised, and trained, as well as rode competitively. "You can't be angry when you're dealing with animals, even when they make you angry. You always have to breathe and deal with it in some kind of way other than losing it."

Importantly, Sandra's beloved nanny also represented critical emotional regulation through her iconic life lessons about facing responsibilities and remaining independent even when you have a valued partner. Implicitly,

Sandra learned that whatever emotions she might be experiencing, she must contain them sufficiently to meet the day with purpose, reliability, and a productive attitude. These lessons bred a steady resilience, self-control, and confidence that she had the equipment to press forward, no matter the challenge or how she felt about it.

Of all my interviewees, Sandra was among the most comfortable with her own anger, displaying a supple ability to harness it and work it to her advantage. This was exquisitely evidenced in the description of her judicial nomination hearing, where she was inwardly furious at the sexist behavior of a colleague who threatened her nomination, but she effectively contained her anger so that it did not derail her desired outcome. Sandra's impressive self-control and constructive use of power and aggression were further honed each day as a courtroom judge whose most critical function is to maintain control within herself and in her courtroom. "When you're angry, you're out of control, and that's not a good thing for a judge."

Sandra displayed two other critical features that furthered her emotional regulation and management of aggression. She was adept at repairing relational ruptures, as seen in her practice of reviewing the day's events with courtroom colleagues over a "cuppa." This was a valued bonding ritual that softened her self-described nastiness. She is also capable of holding opposing perspectives in mind simultaneously. Her relationship with her father displayed this capacity in bold relief; despite her rage at him for multiple serious transgressions, she can also express indebtedness for his excellent care of her deteriorating mother. Rage and gratitude at once, reflecting impressive emotional balance and skill at experiencing multiple points of view.

All in all, Sandra provides a compelling example of a woman whose foundations of love, support, consistency, and work ethic produced a successful woman well in charge of her emotions and strategic about using her aggression productively. "I used my aggression by being stubborn and sticking to the issues without being irate." This is a notable accomplishment, in light of an early environment that, on its face, did not prioritize the naming and managing of emotions.

As I reflect back on my conversation with Shirley to better understand how her home environment intersected with her developing affect regulation and experience of aggression, I notice for the first time that she shared far fewer details about her early life than my other interviewees. Were her feelings regularly noticed by her parents? Was she encouraged to succeed? What about her siblings and the texture and tone of her marriage? Shirley spoke to none of these issues, but what she did offer was that her early home was imbued with memories of her parents' experience in the Holocaust, even though they "spared me their horror stories." We did not delve more deeply into what this all meant, but I intuited that Shirley was describing trauma residue that hovered ominously in the air and defined her life then, just as it does now. Residue that was there but not spoken of. And, like the silent but pervasive shadow of the Holocaust, although my conversation with Shirley lacked significant details, it was nevertheless saturated with intense feelings about her early life in Israel. She spoke movingly about her deep love of her parents, the powerful bond between them, and the weight she carries as the child of parents who lived through and survived the unthinkable.

I wonder if the sparseness of Shirley's narrative reflected some need to protect her family's stories in a shared cocoon of insiders, an effort to seal them off from possible future harm and intrusion given all they had endured. Alternatively, or in addition, much of Shirley's early family story may be dissociated, a dynamic that was hinted at when she told me, "I didn't think it would be so difficult to try to link my early childhood and where I am now, but being an immigrant was part of this equation, I now realize."

There were important qualities about Shirley's early family life that she did say contributed significantly to her emotional sturdiness, such as learning to take nothing for granted and not dwelling on unimportant things. "So, you grow up grateful for the little things. . . . It's better to learn how to prioritize problems early in life." When I inquired if Shirley felt she had to minimize her feelings or manage them alone, since they must have felt miniscule compared to her parents' nightmare, she offered a compelling description of emotional regulation in action:

> It's just a matter of degree. You want to get it out of your system, but you want to put it in perspective. People ask me why I rarely get upset. . . . Because I accept the fact that sometimes things happen the way you want them to, and sometimes they don't.

In addition to her family's Holocaust background, Shirley told me she was profoundly and positively impacted by the cultural norms of her early life in Israel, where one is judged on objective rather than subjective qualities. If you are not the best at everything, it is perfectly acceptable. Shirley believes that Israeli life taught her to focus on goals and results, to do her best at all she attempts, to accept that she will not excel at everything, and to view all feedback as valuable and objective rather than personal. These normative cultural values offered Shirley a textbook education in regulating emotions and mobilizing optimized aggression, an invaluable alternative to her family story of Nazi atrocities.

Shirley's early experiences in the Israeli military provided further practice managing aggression. There, she learned to focus on goals, accept that she cannot control everything, and follow orders regardless of who issues them.

Overall, we might say that through many coalescing influences, Shirley achieved impressive emotional regulation and the ability to robustly strive toward her goals without shame or concern for others. Recall that I was afforded a firsthand experience of her comfort in this regard, when she jauntily offered suggestions to improve my pre-interview questionnaire on leadership and modified my description of how she sees her success. As with Sandra, her comfort in doing so furthered my ability to graciously receive her feedback.

With all that said, however, Shirley still made sure to end our interview by telling me how much she wanted to hear more details about my career change from law to psychology. I believe that her need to refocus onto our relationship likely represented an unconscious need to proactively offset any worries she or I might have that she is an aggressive, nasty woman. In so doing, even a woman as powerful and self-possessed as Shirley was bowing to the patriarchal mandates that sneak into our lives and insidiously judge women's aggression.

Having now completed the exploration of my interviewees' early emotional environments and their effects, I am reminded that we can only speculate about how these issues unfolded in the real moments of everyday life. The stories I was able to create with my interviewees were entirely retrospective and not shared within a therapeutic context, where further inquiry and elaboration could have produced more clarifying information.

What I can safely surmise, however, is that the six women with whom I spoke possessed the resilience and the savvy to capitalize upon the resources they had and to package their affects and aggressive strivings maximally. I know this because each woman looks back upon these functions as key ingredients to her success.

Conclusion

This book has taken as its subject the fraught relationship between women and aggression, one that is burdened by myriad patriarchal norms that reinforce existing power structures by disparaging women's aggressive strivings and mandating their silence. This toxic cultural system sustains itself by hiding in full view, fraudulently passing itself off as natural and even God-given when it decidedly is not. The gravity of this matter is evidenced by its prominence in the political and social discourse of the day, cautionary reminders that our inescapable collusion with patriarchal restrictions must be named and actively challenged if the world is to be made safer and more equitable for women.

In Part I, I took a detailed look inside the sociocultural forces that infect a woman's intrapsychic dynamics and compel her to sacrifice her goals and dreams as she shrinks herself to comply with the cultural demands to be nice, passive, and humble. From three different perspectives—the politics of the day, my own struggles with aggression, and two psychoanalytically oriented clinical vignettes highlighting female aggression—I demonstrated that a woman who acts aggressively today, as throughout history, risks being judged, shamed, and disliked. Even worse, she endangers her most vital relationships.

In Part II, I explored the question of how any woman manages to live a life that includes her robust and creative aggression, given the cultural forces that threaten her. I addressed this critical question through the presentation of psychoanalytically informed interviews with six powerful and influential working women who reached the top of their professions by catalyzing aggression in the service of their goals and thereby disturbing patriarchal inequities. These are women we may ironically describe as "nasty" in only the best sense of the word. They are proof positive that, with the right formula of grit, determination, and resilience, defeating patriarchal barriers and reversing disempowering female symbols like "nasty," is indeed possible. The conversations my interviewees and I created around these issues were rich and illuminating, as much as they were generously and vulnerably offered. I often find myself thinking about these inspiring women in moments when summoning the will to push forward feels beyond reach.

I noted two qualifications about my choice of the working world to demonstrate that women can, in fact, succeed despite patriarchal forces. The first is that achievement in the work environment is only one of many arenas in which a woman can evidence her success, with success broadly understood as the freedom to live by one's own values and follow one's own chosen path, whether working in or outside the home. With that said, I also emphasized the importance of women's ongoing participation in the halls of power and influence, as their involvement counters patriarchal reservations about their leadership capacity, promotes gender equality, and supplies visible models for future female leaders. The second qualification about the work environment as my locus of examination is the need to remember it is not the only setting where women's conflicts with aggression emerge. Rather, these disabling knots rear up in vast corners of women's lives, personal and professional, as most women are well-aware.

The women I chose to interview for this book represent different ethnicities, races, classes, and backgrounds, all of which shaped their paths to success, as did the culture at large, the norms and values of their professions, and the politics of the moment. In other words, the internal and the external will always recursively impact each other, as a woman continually invents and reinvents her own version of power, leadership, and nastiness over her lifetime. This journey will necessitate finding creative ways to flip the liability of being female into an advantage; for example, by transforming existing symbols of female disempowerment into prideworthy badges of honor that are ripe with possibility when skillfully delivered. Exactly how a woman accomplishes this tangled task will lean on her creativity and her determination to succeed.

A series of recurring themes emerged in my six conversations, as my interviewees reflected upon the dynamics and ways of being that they believe have been critical to their success. These included: (1) the consistent presence of loved ones who promoted their self-confidence and inner self-worth; (2) steady emotional regulation that furthered the management of aggression and resilience; (3) a circuitous path to success that optimized positive feedback and inspired the women to continually reach higher; and (4) the deep belief that they were well-suited to their influential positions, although remaining humble about their success was also felt to be essential. I will now review more about each of these features.

Loved ones provided the essential recognition that undergirded each interviewee's belief in herself and her confidence that she could take risks and achieve. These important figures bypassed gender stereotypes and thereby offered permission for each woman not only to dream big, but also to actualize her goals with grit and pride. One interviewee, who lacked the steady presence of affirming loved ones in her early home, purposefully sought out other relationships and experiences that offered the support and recognition she was missing—local businesspeople who valued her abilities, the church, and a life-changing psychoanalysis that repaired her view of herself. Relational support and recognition also fueled each woman's determination to overcome patriarchal threats, which were unanimously acknowledged but skillfully sidestepped with humor and letting them pass. These soft approaches to quelling sexism were felt to be justified, as the women viewed success as the best revenge, rather than reactivity or victimhood, which could compromise their goals. I discussed the possible risks and benefits of dealing with sexism in these indirect ways; that is, whether such an approach constitutes a capitulation to misogynistic behavior, or, in contrast, a creative form of aggression that effectively defeats male attempts to objectify and thwart women.

Steady emotional regulation that promoted the effective management of aggression, particularly anger, was also consistently cited as critical to each woman's success, whether navigating racism and sexism, a challenging freshman year at college, a new American culture, an explosive father, a deceitful father, or a critical, depressed mother. For my Black interviewee, the ability to contain aggression was felt to be particularly essential, given the known double jeopardy of sexism and racism that haunts Black women. For the one woman whose early home life was dominated by her father's unregulated rage and her mother's passive aggressiveness, it was her analyst and a supportive husband who helped her reclaim her aggression as an essential part of self. The remaining women felt they had learned to regulate their anger and other emotions from parents who had modeled the successful management of these complex feelings.

There was one curious finding in my interviews that related to the question of emotional regulation; that is, all interviewees described their early homes as lacking meaningful discussions of feelings and discomfort with most outward displays of affection. I explored whether such a situation necessarily leaves a negative trace on children and complicates their relationship to emotional regulation and aggression, since psychoanalytic psychotherapists know that "being able to share your deepest pain and deepest feelings with another human being . . . is one of the most profound experiences we can have" (Van der Kolk, 2014, p. 237), and we entrust words and verbal reflection to handle this job. How then do we make sense of the sparse emotional environments in these six stories?

We do know from the psychoanalytic literature that words themselves are only one possible way for parents to communicate attunement, confidence, and encouragement to their children. Others include encouraging a young girl's growing achievement and abilities and helping her transcend limiting gender stereotypes. But I also considered the potential negative impact of a home that discourages the meaningful discussion of feelings. A child may, as a result, seal off her emotions and dissociate her aggression, thereby sacrificing essential parts of herself. Or she may struggle in her relationships when conflicts arise without earlier experiences of owning her aggression and repairing ruptures. These risks were ultimately difficult to fully assess for two reasons: the majority of my interviewees were resolute that their early environments were loving and supportive despite their lack of emotional conversations, and our discussions focused primarily on success in the workplace rather than women's relational worlds. What I have comfortably concluded, however, is that, even without early experiences of actively sharing their internal worlds, these women developed the resilience and savvy to capitalize upon the resources they had and to constructively package their emotions and strivings in ways well-suited to their particular professional contexts.

Returning now to the recurring themes in my interviews, none of the career trajectories discussed were straightforward or imagined early on. Visions and goals for the future among these women were notably modest when they were young, but they gradually grew as the women leveraged positive opportunities and internalized mentors who viewed them as talented and capable. Though most of the women were surprised where they ultimately landed, once there, they understood why, knowing they had what it took to succeed.

All six women I interviewed described the importance of remaining humble and soft-spoken about their significant accomplishments despite their deep pride in them. Whether because they viewed their success as primarily a matter of lucky circumstances or an indispensable husband, or whether their family and cultural surround frowned upon showiness of any kind, it was essential not to get "puffed up" about any of it. One woman went as far as explaining that, notwithstanding her pride about her powerful position, she does not think of herself as ambitious or driven at all. This may reflect the understandable fear any woman has about being perceived as aggressive, as well as her likely view of aggression as a force that only causes damage, rather than one with positive and empowering dimensions as well.

In a related fashion, all six women remarked how much they enjoyed the chance to tell me their story, but also how awkward it felt to talk about themselves for such a lengthy period. One woman of great talent and success even remarked how surprised she was that she was selected to do so. Much of this emphasis on humility or, in one case, the outright dissociation of drive and ambition, struck me as an unconscious salute to the dominant culture's warning that a woman should not be overly powerful, angry, or strong—even when she evidently is.

When all is said and done, we are left to accept that women must navigate an impossibly narrow tightrope as they step out aggressively toward success, and even well after they have arrived. As many women know, "it's hard to be a difficult woman" (Turkle, 2021, p. 328) and to feel comfortable in one's own skin as a powerful female leader. But, as even the highest-ranking female CEO in the Fortune 500[1] wisely advises: "There's always going to be those little voices in your head saying, *You can't do this* or questioning it. And you've just got to push beyond those voices and say, *Yes, I can*" (Aiyengar, 2022–present). For we cannot afford to risk losing women's distinctive voices representing half of all knowledge (Reciniello, 2011) by marginalizing them. After all,

there is something quintessentially human about the voice (Karp, 2006) . . . the personal instrument we use to make things happen in our lives—to effect change, to create and to love. Let it founder and we rob ourselves of the ability to touch others and leave our mark on the world. Let it soar and we enrich our sense of who we are and who we can be, stepping out to create lives of meaning and fulfillment.

(Zuckerman, 2014b, p. 280)

When women dare to defy the patriarchy, speak out, and ascend, their voices become vehicles of resistance (Gilligan, 2020) that accomplish essential things. They degender basic human traits, such as assertiveness, anger, and relationality; nourish the aspirations of the next generation; counteract doubts about women's leadership capacity (S. D. O'Connor, 2007); and live as balanced human beings without concern for what gender is involved (Williams & Dempsey, 2014). They also succeed in transforming toxic tropes such as nastiness and bitchiness into essential qualities that will always accompany a woman who leaves a lasting and meaningful imprint upon the world. For, as Tina Fey cogently observes, "you know what? Bitches get stuff done" (Williams & Dempsey, 2014, p. 74). My great hope is that this book will provide pathways and inspiration for women to step out and reclaim their once-owned nastiness, reimagining it as a revitalized part of themselves that holds limitless possibilities.

Note

1 Karen Lynch is the CEO and president of CVS Health.

References

Adichie, C. N. (2015). *We should all be feminists*. Anchor Books.

Aiyengar, A. (Host). (2022, December). A commitment to mental and physical health spelled success for CVS Health CEO Karen Lynch. [Audio podcast episode.] In *Women on the Move Podcast*. https://open.spotify.com/episode/0uWAYRHdubV1gPkbD6pQZ2?si=7ykYQYSVQF-SWztVpVPH0A&nd=1&dlsi=bd2a01cf9af847a4.

Atlas, G. (2015). Touch me, know me: The enigma of erotic longing. *Psychoanalytic Psychology, 32*(1), 123–139. https://doi.org/10.1037/a0037182.

Atlas, G., & Aron, L. (2017). *Dramatic dialogues: Contemporary clinical practice*. Routledge. http://dx.doi.org/10.4324/9781315150086.

Baker-Pitts, C. (2014). Still dangerous: Women and public speaking. *Psychoanalytic Perspectives, 11*(3), 294–305. http://dx.doi.org/10.1080/1551806X.2014.938954.

Barrett, L. F. (2016, September 23). Hillary Clinton's "angry" face. *The New York Times*. https://www.nytimes.com/2016/09/25/opinion/sunday/hillary-clintons-angry-face.html.

Barth, F. D. (2018). With friends like these, who needs enemies? Split off, "not me" competitive strivings in women's friendships and sense of self. *Psychoanalytic Dialogues, 28*(4), 432–445. http://dx.doi.org/10.1080/10481885.2018.1482143.

Beard, M. (2017). *Women & power: A manifesto*. W. W. Norton & Company.

Beard, M. (2018, February 17). Oxfam. *The Times Literary Supplement*. https://www.the-tls.co.uk/oxfam/.

Benjamin, J. (1991). Father and daughter: Identification with difference—A contribution to gender heterodoxy. *Psychoanalytic Dialogues, 1*(3), 277–299. http://dx.doi.org/10.1080/10481889109538900.

Benjamin, J. (2005). From many into one: Attention, energy, and the containing of multitudes. *Psychoanalytic Dialogues, 15*(2), 185–201. http://dx.doi.org/10.1080/10481881509348826.

Benjamin, J. (2017). *Beyond doer and done to: Recognition theory, intersubjectivity and the third*. Routledge. http://dx.doi.org/10.4324/9781315437699.

Bennett, J. (2018, September 28). The "tight rope" of testifying while female. *The New York Times*. https://www.nytimes.com/2018/09/28/us/politics/christine-blasey-ford-testimony-testifying-while-female.html.

Bennett, J. (2019, November 20). What do we hear when women speak? *The New York Times*. http://www.nytimes.com/2019/11/20/us/politics/women-voices-authority.html.

Bennett, J. (2023, November 13). Maybe this is why Donald Trump is afraid to debate Nikki Haley. *The New York Times*. https://www.nytimes.com/2023/11/13/opinion/nikki-haley-high-heels.html.

Bennett, J. (2024, February 1). "Mean Girls" has lost its bite. Girls haven't. *The New York Times*. https://www.nytimes.com/2024/02/01/opinion/mean-girls-movie-bullying.html.

Ben-Noam, S. (2018). Cracking the intrapsychic "glass ceiling" for women in leadership: Therapeutic interventions. *Psychoanalytic Inquiry*, *38*(4), 299–311. https://doi.org/10.1080/07351690.2018.1444856.

Billingsley, A. (2019). *Humorwork, feminist philosophy, and unstable politics*. [Doctoral dissertation, University of Oregon.] Scholars' Bank. http://hdl.handle.net/1794/24550.

Blow, C. M. (2024, January 3). The persecution of Harvard's Claudine Gay. *The New York Times*. https://www.nytimes.com/2024/01/03/opinion/harvard-claudine-gay-politics.html?smid=nytcore-ios-share&referringSource=articleShare.

Boston Change Process Study Group, The. (2010). *Change processes in psychotherapy: A unifying paradigm*. W. W. Norton & Company.

Boston Globe, The. (2023, November 10). *It's time to bring Middle East studies into college classrooms*. https://www.bostonglobe.com/2023/11/12/opinion/israel-palestine-college-classrooms/.

Bromberg, P. M. (1998). *Standing in the spaces: Essays on clinical process trauma, and dissociation*. Analytic Press.

Bromberg, P. M. (2000). Potholes on the royal road: Or is it an abyss? *Contemporary Psychoanalysis*, *36*(1), 5–28. http://dx.doi.org/10.1080/00107530.2000.10747043.

Bromberg, P. M. (with Schore, A.). (2011). *The shadow of the tsunami: And the growth of the relational mind*. Routledge.

Brown, L. M., & Gilligan, C. (1992). *Meeting at the crossroads: Women's psychology and girls' development*. Harvard University Press. http://dx.doi.org/10.4159/harvard.9780674731837.

Bruni, F. (2017, April 1). Manhood in the age of Trump. *The New York Times*. https://www.nytimes.com/2017/04/01/opinion/sunday/manhood-in-the-age-of-trump.html.

Buchanan, K. (2023, November 26). Beyoncé's "Renaissance" film: 4 takeaways from the premiere. *The New York Times*. https://www.nytimes.com/2023/11/26/movies/beyonce-renaissance-premiere-film.html.

Bueskens, P. (Ed.). (2021). *Nancy Chodorow and the reproduction of mothering, 40 years on*. Palgrave Macmillan.

Campbell, A. (1993). *Men, women and aggression*. Basic Books.

Caperhart, J. (2023, March 4). Doug Emhoff is the antidote to toxic masculinity. *The Washington Post*. https://www.washingtonpost.com/opinions/2023/03/04/douglas-emhoff-kamala-harris-toxic-masculinity/.

Chess, S. (2021, April 1). The lulz of Medusa: On laughter as protest. *The MIT Press Reader*. https://thereader.mitpress.mit.edu/the-lulz-of-medusa-on-laughter-as-protest/.

Chira, S. (2017a, June 26). Nancy Pelosi, Washington's latest wicked witch. *The New York Times*. https://www.nytimes.com/2017/06/26/opinion/nancy-pelosi-washingtons-latest-wicked-witch.html.

Chira, S. (2017b, July 21). Why women aren't CEO's, according to women who almost were. *The New York Times*. https://www.nytimes.com/2017/07/21/sunday-review/women-ceos-glass-ceiling.html.

Chodorow, N. J. (1978). *The reproduction of mothering: Psychoanalysis and the sociology of gender*. University of California Press. http://dx.doi.org/10.1525/9780520924086.

Chodorow, N. J. (1995). Gender as a personal and cultural construction. *Signs*, *20*(3), 516–544. http://dx.doi.org/10.1086/494999.

Chodorow, N. J. (2011). *Individualizing gender and sexuality: Theory and practice*. Routledge. http://dx.doi.org/10.4324/9780203816066.

Clinton, H. R. (2017). *What happened*. Simon & Schuster.

Coates, S. W. (1998). Having a mind of one's own and holding the other in mind: Commentary on paper by Peter Fonagy and Mary Target. *Psychoanalytic Dialogues, 8*(1), 115–148. http://dx.doi.org/10.1080/10481889809539236.

Cohut, M. (2020, October 13). The controversy of "female hysteria." *Medical News Today*. https://www.medicalnewstoday.com/articles/the-controversy-of-female-hysteria.

Cottle, M. (2022, November 17). Nancy Pelosi, badass. *The New York Times*. https://www.nytimes.com/2022/11/17/opinion/pelosi-speaker.html.

Crastnopol, M. (2018). Unpacking competitiveness within and between women: Discussion of "With friends like these, who needs enemies?" *Psychoanalytic Dialogues, 28*(4), 446–454. http://dx.doi.org/10.1080/10481885.2018.1482144.

Crosby, R. L., & Edwards, J. B. (2021). Why people lead and others follow: The Black perspective. *Psychoanalytic Inquiry, 41*(7), 509–526. https://doi.org/10.1080/07351690.2021.1971468.

deBoer, F. (2023). *How elites ate the social justice movement*. Simon & Shuster.

D'Ercole, A. (2023). *Clara M. Thompson's early years and professional awakening: An American psychoanalyst (1893–1933)*. Routledge. http://dx.doi.org/10.4324/9781003261797.

Devereux, C. (2014). Hysteria, feminism, and gender revisited: The case of the second wave. *ESC: English Studies in Canada, 40*(1), 19–45. https://doi.org/10.1353/esc.2014.0004.

Diller, V. (2014). The new beauty paradox. In N. D. O'Reilly (Ed.), *Leading women: 20 influential women share their secrets to leadership, business, and life* (pp. 119–127). Simon & Schuster.

Dimen, M. (1991). Deconstructing difference: Gender, splitting, and transitional space. *Psychoanalytic Dialogues, 1*(3), 335–352. http://dx.doi.org/10.1080/10481889109538904.

Dimen, M. (2003). *Sexuality, intimacy, power*. Routledge.

Dinnerstein, D. (1976). *The mermaid and the minotaur*. Harper & Row.

Dowd, M. (2023a, September 30). DiFi, breaking into the boys' club. *The New York Times*. https://www.nytimes.com/2023/09/30/opinion/dianne-feinstein-boys-club.html.

Dowd, M. (2023b, October 7). Travis, don't fumble Taylor! *The New York Times*. https://www.hanytimes.com/2023/10/07/opinion/taylor-swift-travis-kelce-fame.html.

Drexler, P. (2014, July 22). How women define success. *Forbes*. https://www.forbes.com/sites/peggydrexler/2014/07/22/how-women-define-success/.

Eagly, A. H. (2020). *Once more: The rise of female leaders: How gender and ethnicity affect the electability and success of women as political leaders*. [Research brief.] American Psychological Association. https://www.apa.org/topics/women-girls/female-leaders.

Elise, D. (2008). Sex and shame: The inhibition of female desires. *Journal of the American Psychoanalytic Association, 56*(1), 73–98. http://dx.doi.org/10.1177/0003065108315685.

Esposito, J. E. (2000). *In the spotlight: Overcoming your fear of public speaking and performing*. Strong Books—Publishing Directions, LLC.

Fahy, C. (2023, October 10). Saying goodbye to a San Francisco icon. *The New York Times*. https://www.nytimes.com/2023/10/10/us/dianne-feinstein-san-francisco.html.

Feldt, G. (2014). From oppression to leadership: Women redefine power. In N. D. O'Reilly (Ed.), *Leading women: 20 influential women share their secrets to leadership, business, and life* (pp. 17–24). Simon & Schuster.

Ferenczi, S. (1955). Confusion of tongues between adults and the child. In S. Ferenczi, *Final contributions to the problems and methods of psychoanalysis* (M. Balint, Ed., E. Mosbacher et al., Trans., pp. 156–167). Hogarth.

Filipovic, J. (2017, November 24). The bad news on "good" girls. *The New York Times*. https://www.nytimes.com/2017/11/24/opinion/sunday/girls-parents-boys-gender.html.

Frankel, L. (2015). Eight key ways women become natural and necessary leaders. In N. D. O'Reilly (Ed.), *Leading women: 20 influential women share their secrets to leadership, business, and life* (pp. 45–52). Simon & Schuster.

Freeman, H. (2013, April 9). Margaret Thatcher was no feminist. *The Guardian.* https://www.theguardian.com/commentisfree/2013/apr/09/margaret-thatcher-no-feminist.

Freeman, J. (1972). The tyranny of the structurelessness. *The Second Wave, 2,* 20.

Freud, S. (1909). 'Analysis of a phobia in a five-year-old boy.' *The Standard Edition, X,* 140.

Freud, S. (1920). Beyond the pleasure principle. *The Standard Edition, 18,* 1–64.

Fromm, E. (1964). *The heart of man: Its genius for good and evil.* Harper & Row.

Ganesan, S. (2016, August 17). What do women leaders have in common? *The Atlantic.* https://www.theatlantic.com/business/archive/2016/08/what-do-women-leaders-have-in-common/492656/.

Garfield, R. (2003). Aggression and women. *Journal of the American Psychoanalytic Association, 51*(2), 637–649. http://dx.doi.org/10.1177/00030651030510020401.

Gentile, J. (2022). On psychoanalysis's invention of patriarchy and the democratic significance of anatomical difference. In J. Petrucelli, S. Schoen, & N. Snider (Eds.), *Patriarchy and its discontents: Psychoanalytic perspectives* (pp. 110–131). Routledge. http://dx.doi.org/10.4324/9781003262299-9.

Gilligan, C. (1982). *In a different voice: Psychological theory and women's development.* Harvard University Press.

Gilligan, C. (2004). Recovering psyche: Reflections on life-history and history. In J. A. Winer & J. W. Anderson (Eds.), *The annual of psychoanalysis: Psychoanalysis and women* (Vol. 32, pp. 131–147). Routledge.

Gilligan, C. (2020). Disrupting the story: Enter Eve. *Journal of the American Psychoanalytic Association, 68*(4), 675–693. http://dx.doi.org/10.1177/0003065120950434.

Gilligan, C., Lyons, N. P., & Hanmer T. J. (1990). *Making connections: The relational worlds of adolescent girls at Emma Willard School.* Harvard University Press.

Gilligan, C., & Snider, N. (2017). The loss of pleasure, or why we are still talking about Oedipus. *Contemporary Psychoanalysis, 53*(2), 173–195. http://dx.doi.org/10.1080/00107530.2017.1310586.

Gilligan, C., & Snider, N. (2018). *Why does patriarchy persist?* Polity Press.

Gino, F., Wilmuth, C. A., & Brooks, A. W. (2015, September 21). Compared to men, women view professional advancement as equally attainable, but less desirable. *Proceedings of the National Academy of Sciences, 112*(40), 12354–12359. https://doi.org/10.1073/pnas.1502567112.

Glueck, K., & Lerer, L. (2023, February 19). Haley walks treacherous road for G.O.P. women. *The New York Times.* https://www.nytimes.com/2020/05/19/us/politics/biden-vice-president-trump.html.

Goldberg, E. (2022, June 2). What Sheryl Sandberg's 'Lean In' has meant to women. *The New York Times.* https://www.nytimes.com/2022/06/02/business/sheryl-sandberg-lean-in.html.

Grant, A. (2023, July 31). Women know exactly what they're doing when they use "weak language." *The New York Times.* https://www.nytimes.com/2023/07/31/opinion/women-language-work.html.

Greenhouse, L. (2020, September 18). Ruth Bader Ginsberg, Supreme Court's feminist icon, is dead at 87. *The New York Times.* https://www.nytimes.com/2020/09/18/us/ruth-bader-ginsburg-dead.html.

Greenhouse, L. (2023, December 1). Sandra Day O'Connor, first woman on the Supreme Court, is dead at 93. *The New York Times*. https://www.nytimes.com/2023/12/01/us/sandra-day-oconnor-dead.html.

Grundy, D. (1993). Parricide postponed: A discussion of some writing problems. *Contemporary Psychoanalysis, 29*(4), 693–710.

Harris, A. (1997). Aggression, envy, and ambition: Circulating tensions in women's psychic life. *Gender & Psychoanalysis, 2*(3), 291–325.

Harris, A. (1998). Aggression: Pleasures and dangers. *Psychoanalytic Inquiry, 18*, 31–44.

Harris, A. (2002). Mothers, monsters, mentors. *Studies in Gender and Sexuality, 3*(3), 281–295. http://dx.doi.org/10.1080/15240650309349201.

Harris, A. (2014). Curative speech: Symbol, body, dialogue. *Journal of the American Psychoanalytic Association, 62*(6), 1029–1045. http://dx.doi.org/10.1177/0003065114557863.

Helgerson, S. (2018, April 13). How women define success. *How Women Rise*. https://www.howwomenrise.com/how-women-define-success/.

Hirsch, I. (1993). Countertransference enactments and some issues related to external factors in the analyst's life. *Psychoanalytic Dialogues, 3*(3), 343–366. http://dx.doi.org/10.1080/10481889309538980.

Hirsch, I. (1996). Observing-participation, mutual enactment, and the new classical models. *Contemporary Psychoanalysis, 32*(3), 359–383. http://dx.doi.org/10.1080/00107530.1996.10746958.

Hirsch, I. (2008a). *Coasting in the countertransference: Conflicts of self-interest between analyst and patient*. Routledge. http://dx.doi.org/10.4324/9780203927274.

Hirsch, I. (2008b). Introduction. In D. B. Stern & I. Hirsch (Eds.), *Further developments in interpersonal psychoanalysis, 1980s through 2010s* (pp. 1–9). Routledge.

Hirsch, I. (2011). On some contributions of the interpersonal psychoanalytic tradition to 21st-century psychoanalysis. *Contemporary Psychoanalysis, 47*(4), 561–570. http://dx.doi.org/10.1080/00107530.2011.10746479.

Holmes, D. E. (2021). "I do not have a racist bone in my body": Psychoanalytic perspectives on what is lost and not mourned in our culture's persistent racism. *Journal of the American Psychoanalytic Association, 69*(2), 237–258. https://doi.org/10.1177/0003065121100958.

Johnson, S. K., Murphy, S. E., Zewdie, S., & Reichard, R. J. (2008). The strong, sensitive type: Effects of gender stereotypes and leadership prototypes on the evaluation of male and female leaders. *Organizational Behavior and Human Decision Processes, 106*(1), 39–60. http://dx.doi.org/10.1016/j.obhdp.2007.12.002.

Johnston, E. (2016). The original "nasty woman." *The Atlantic*. https://www.theatlantic.com/entertainment/archive/2016/11/the-original-nasty-woman-of-classical-myth/506591/.

Keohane, N. (2007). Crossing the bridge: Reflections on women and leadership. In B. Kellerman & D. Rhode (Eds.), *Women and leadership: The state of play and strategies for change* (pp. 1–62). Jossey-Bass.

Kernberg, O. F. (1991). Aggression and love in the relationship of the couple. *Journal of the American Psychoanalytic Association, 39*(1), 45–70. http://dx.doi.org/10.1177/000306519103900103.

Kirshner, L. A. (2014). Raids on the unsayable: Talk in psychoanalysis. *Journal of the American Psychoanalytic Association, 62*(6), 1047–1061. http://dx.doi.org/10.1177/0003065114559943.

Klemesrud, J. (1985, August 9). Women in the law: Many are getting out. *The New York Times*. https://www.nytimes.com/1985/08/09/style/women-in-the-law-many-are-getting-out.html.

Knox, J. (2013). The mind in fragments: The neuroscientific, developmental, and traumatic roots of dissociation and their implications for clinical practice. *Psychoanalytic Inquiry, 33*(5), 449–466. http://dx.doi.org/10.1080/07351690.2013.815063.

Kohut, H. (1972). Thoughts on narcissism and narcissistic rage. *The Psychoanalytic Study of the Child, 27*(1), 360–400. http://dx.doi.org/10.1080/00797308.1972.11822721.

Kolod, S. (2017). Trump world: What do women want? *Contemporary Psychoanalysis, 53*(4), 567–582. http://dx.doi.org/10.1080/00107530.2017.1381874.

Kring, A. M. (2000). Gender and anger. In A. H. Fischer (Ed.), *Gender and emotion: Social psychological perspectives* (pp. 211–231). Cambridge University Press. http://dx.doi.org/10.1017/CBO9780511628191.011.

Layton, L. (2020). *Toward a social psychoanalysis: Culture, character, and normative unconscious processes* (M. Leavy-Sperounis, Ed.). Routledge. http://dx.doi.org/10.4324/9781003023098.

Layton, L., & Redman, P. (2017). Gratitude and leave-taking: Editorial reflections, 2013–2017. *Psychoanalysis, Culture and Society, 22*, 347–363.

Leibovich, M. (2020, May 19). The end of "who me? For V.P." Politics. *The New York Times.* https://www.nytimes.com/2020/05/19/us/politics/biden-vice-president-trump.html.

Lerner, H. E. (1980). Internal prohibitions against female anger. *The American Journal of Psychoanalysis, 40*, 137–148. http://dx.doi.org/10.1007/BF01254806.

Levenson, E. (1983). *The ambiguity of change: An inquiry into the nature of psychoanalytic reality.* Basic Books.

Levenson, E. A. (1984). Harry Stack Sullivan: The web and the spider. *Contemporary Psychoanalysis, 20*(2), 174–189. https://doi.org/10.1080/00107530.1984.10745726.

Levenson, E. A. (1996). The politics of interpretation. *Contemporary Psychoanalysis, 32*(4), 631–648. http://dx.doi.org/10.1080/00107530.1996.10746341.

Lionells, M., Fiscalini, J., Mann, C., & Stern, D. B. (1996). *Handbook of interpersonal psychoanalysis.* Routledge. http://dx.doi.org/10.4324/9781315803432.

Liptak, A. (2017, April 17). Why Gorsuch may not be so genteel on the bench. *The New York Times.* https://www.nytimes.com/2012/10/18/opinion/in-the-debates-interruption-or-interjection.html.

Litowitz, B. E. (2011). From dyad to dialogue: Language and the early relationship in American psychoanalytic theory. *Journal of the American Psychoanalytic Association, 59*(3), 483–507. http://dx.doi.org/10.1177/0003065111406440.

Litowitz, B. E. (2014). Coming to terms with intersubjectivity: Keeping language in mind. *Journal of the American Psychoanalytic Association, 62*(2), 295–312. http://dx.doi.org/10.1177/0003065114530156.

Loewald, H. W. (1979). The waning of the Oedipus complex. *Journal of the American Psychoanalytic Association, 27*(4), 751–775. http://dx.doi.org/10.1177/000306517902700401.

Loewald, H. W. (with Lear, J.). (2000). *The essential Loewald: Collected papers and monographs.* University Publishing Group.

Lorde, A. (1981). The uses of anger. *Women's Studies Quarterly, 9*(3), 7–10. https://academicworks.cuny.edu/wsq/509/.

Maccoby, M. (2021). Leadership in context. *Psychoanalytic Inquiry, 41*(7), 446–455.

Margolies, J. (2023, November 11). A Black woman's rise in architecture shows how far is left to go. *The New York Times.* https://www.nytimes.com/2023/11/11/business/architecture-diversity-black-women.html.

Masten, A. (2001). Ordinary magic: Resilience processes in development. *American Psychologist, 56*(3), 227–238. https://doi.org/10.1037/0003-066X.56.3.227.

Miller, K. (2023, August 1). Move over, men: Women were hunters, too. *The New York Times*. https://www.nytimes.com/2023/08/01/science/anthropology-women-hunting.html.

Millett, K. (1970). *Sexual politics*. Doubleday.

Obama, M. (2018). *Becoming*. Crown.

O'Connor, R. (2018, February 18). Mary Beard posts tearful picture of herself after defence of Oxfam aid workers provokes backlash. *The Independent*. https://www.independent.co.uk/news/uk/home-news/mary-beard-tweet-oxfam-aid-workers-sex-scandal-backlash-feminists-cambridge-priyamvada-gopal-latest a8216306.html.

O'Connor, S. D. (2007). Foreword. In B. Kellerman & D. Rhode (Eds.), *Women and leadership: The state of play and strategies for change* (pp. xiii–xv). Jossey-Bass.

Ogden. T. H. (1997). Some thoughts on the use of language in psychoanalysis. *Psychoanalytic Dialogues*, *7*(1), 1–21. http://dx.doi.org/10.1080/10481889709539164.

Ogden. T. H. (1998). A question of voice in poetry and psychoanalysis. *The Psychoanalytic Quarterly*, *67*(3), 426–448. http://dx.doi.org/10.1080/00332828.1998.12006050.

Ogden, T. H. (1999). "The music of what happens" in poetry and psychoanalysis. *The International Journal of Psychoanalysis*, *80*, 979–994.

Ogden, T. H. (2016). On language and truth in psychoanalysis. *The Psychoanalytic Quarterly*, *85*(2), 411–426. http://dx.doi.org/10.1002/psaq.12079.

Ogden, T. H. (2021). *Coming to life in the consulting room: Toward a new analytic sensibility*. Routledge. http://dx.doi.org/10.4324/9781003228462.

Olusoga, D. (2017, August 12). Black people have had a presence in our history for centuries. Get over it. *The Guardian*. https://www.theguardian.com/commentisfree/2017/aug/12/black-people-presence-in-british-history-for-centuries.

Patchett, A. (2023). *Tom Lake*. Harper.

Person, E. (1982). Women working. *Journal of the Academy of Psychoanalysis and Dynamic Psychiatry*, *10*, 67–84.

Phillips, L. (2015). The power of the podium: Challenges and opportunities to be seen and heard. In N. D. O'Reilly (Ed.), *Leading women: 20 influential women share their secrets to leadership, business, and life* (pp. 25–35). Simon & Schuster.

Pipher, M. (1994). *Reviving Ophelia: Saving the selves of adolescent girls*. Riverhead.

Pittinsky, T., Bacon, L., & Welle, B. (2007). The great women theory of leadership? Perils of positive stereotypes and precarious pedestals. In B. Kellerman & D. Rhode (Eds.), *Women and leadership: The state of play and strategies for change* (pp. 93–125). Jossey-Bass.

Pizer, B. (2003). When the crunch is a (k)not: A crimp in relational dialogue. *Psychoanalytic Dialogues*, *13*(2), 171–192. http://dx.doi.org/10.1080/10481881309348727.

Radke, H. R. M., Hornsey, M. J., & Barlow, F. K. (2016). Barriers to women engaging in collective action to overcome sexism. *American Psychologist*, *71*(9), 863–874. https://doi.org/10.1037/a0040345.

Reciniello, S. (2011). Is woman the future of man? An exploration of the potential of women in the knowledge economy and of the problem of gender inequality in the workplace. *Organizational and Social Dynamics*, *2*, 151–174. http://dx.doi.org/10.33212/osd.v11n2.2011.151.

Reckling. A. E., & Buirski, P. (1996). Child abuse, self-development, and affect regulation. *Psychoanalytic Psychology*, *13*(1), 81–99. http://dx.doi.org/10.1037/h0079639.

Regine, B. (2015). Soft is the new hard: The hidden power of feminine skills. In N. D. O'Reilly (Ed.), *Leading women: 20 influential women share their secrets to leadership, business, and life* (pp. 53–60). Simon & Schuster.

Reynolds, M. (2015). The burden of greatness. In N. D. O'Reilly (Ed.), *Leading women: 20 influential women share their secrets to leadership, business, and life* (pp. 97–101). Simon & Schuster.

Rhode, D., & Kellerman, B. (2007). Women and leadership: The state of play. In B. Kellerman & D. Rhode (Eds.), *Women and leadership: The state of play and strategies for change* (pp. 1–62). Jossey-Bass.

Riddell, K. (2016, January 14). Hillary Clinton haunted by efforts to "destroy" Bill Clinton accusers. *The Washington Times.* https://www.washingtontimes.com/news/2016/jan/14/hillary-clinton-haunted-by-efforts-to-destroy-bill/.

Ro, C. (2024, February 18). *How to improve your sense of direction.* BBC. https://www.bbc.com/future/article/20240215-do-some-people-have-a-better-sense-of-direction.

Rozmarin, E. (2017). The social is the unconscious of the unconscious of psychoanalysis. *Contemporary Psychoanalysis, 53*(4), 459–469. http://dx.doi.org/10.1080/00107530.2017.1385373.

Sageman, S. (2004). Commentary on "The hand that rocks the cradle rocks the boat: The empowerment of women" by Ann Ruth Turkel. *The Journal of the Academy of Psychoanalysis and Dynamic Psychiatry, 32*(1), 55–57. https://doi.org/10.1521/jaap.32.1.55.28322.

Saketopoulou, A. (2023). *Sexuality beyond consent: Risk, race, traumatophilia.* New York University Press. http://dx.doi.org/10.18574/nyu/9781479820276.001.0001.

Salerno, J. M., Phalen, H. J., Reyes, R. N., & Schweitzer, N. J. (2018). Closing with emotion: The differential impact of male versus female attorneys expressing anger in court. *Law and Human Behavior, 42*(4), 385–401. http://dx.doi.org/10.1037/lhb0000292.

Sandberg, S. (2010, December). *Why we have too few women leaders.* [Video.] TED Conferences. https://www.ted.com/talks/sheryl_sandberg_why_we_have_too_few_women_leaders/transcript.

Sandberg, S. (2013). *Lean in.* Knopf.

Schneier, M. (2016, April 16). Mary Beard and her "battle cry" against internet trolling. *The New York Times.* https://www.nytimes.com/2016/04/17/fashion/mary-beard-against-internet-trolling.html.

Schore, A. (2011). The right brain implicit self lies at the core of psychoanalysis. *Psychoanalytic Dialogues, 21*(1), 75–100. https://doi.org/10.1080/10481885.2011.545329.

Seligman, S. (2022). Patriarchy in psychoanalytic theory and organizations: The Oedipus complex as ideology. In J. Petrucelli, S. Schoen, & N. Snider (Eds.), *Patriarchy and its discontents: Psychoanalytic perspectives* (pp. 49–75). Routledge.

Seligson, H. (2024, January 12). When mean girls grow up. *The New York Times.* https://www.nytimes.com/2024/01/12/style/mean-girls-rosalind-wiseman.html.

Simmons, R. (2002). *Odd girl out: The hidden culture of aggression in girls.* Mariner Books.

Slochower, J. (1998). Illusion and uncertainty in psychoanalytic writing. *International Journal of Psychoanalysis, 79*(2), 333–347.

Spivak, A. P. (2014). The interpretive process: The power of "mere" words. *Journal of the American Psychoanalytic Association, 62*(6), 1063–1073. http://dx.doi.org/10.1177/0003065114558516.

Stern, D. B. (1997). *Unformulated experience: From dissociation to imagination in psychoanalysis.* Analytic Press.

Stern, D. B. (2004). The eye sees itself. *Contemporary Psychoanalysis, 40*(2), 197–237. http://dx.doi.org/10.1080/00107530.2004.10745828.

Stern, D. B. (2009). *Partners in thought: Working with unformulated experience, dissociation, and enactment.* Routledge. http://dx.doi.org/10.4324/9780203880388.

Stern, D. B. (2015). *Relational freedom: Emergent properties of the interpersonal field.* Routledge. http://dx.doi.org/10.4324/9781315765570.

Stern, D. B. (2019). *The infinity of the unsaid: Unformulated experience, language, and the nonverbal.* Routledge. http://dx.doi.org/10.4324/9780429468087.

Stern, D. B. (2022). On coming into possession of oneself: Witnessing and the formulation of experience. *The Psychoanalytic Quarterly, 91*(4), 639–667. http://dx.doi.org/10.1080/00332828.2022.2153528.

Stern, D. B. (2023). Commentary on Markham's vignette. *Journal of the American Psychoanalytic Association, 71*, 113–118.

Stern, D. N. (1985). *The interpersonal world of the infant: A view from psychoanalysis and developmental psychology.* Basic Books. http://dx.doi.org/10.4324/9780429482137.

Stoller, R. J. (1979). *Sexual excitement: Dynamics of erotic life.* Pantheon. http://dx.doi.org/10.4324/9780429480041.

Sullivan, H. S. (Ed.). (1953). *The interpersonal theory of psychiatry.* W. W. Norton & Company. http://dx.doi.org/10.4324/9781315014029.

Suryani, L. K. (2004). Balinese women in a changing society. *The Journal of the American Academy of Psychoanalysis and Dynamic Psychiatry, 32*(1), 213–230. http://dx.doi.org/10.1521/jaap.32.1.213.28335.

Taylor, J. M., Gilligan, C., & Sullivan, A. M. (1995). *Between voice and silence: Women and girls, race and relationship.* Harvard University Press.

Thomas, E. (2023, December 1). The keys to O'Conner's power? Civility and self-restraint. *The Washington Post.* https://www.washingtonpost.com/opinions/2023/12/01/sandra-day-oconnor-civility-restraint/.

Thompson, C. (1958). Concepts of the self in interpersonal theory. *The American Journal of Psychotherapy, 12*(1), 5–17. http://dx.doi.org/10.1176/appi.psychotherapy.1958.12.1.5.

Tosone, C. (2009). *Sotto voce*: Internalized misogyny and the politics of gender in corporate America. *Psychoanalytic Social Work, 16*, 1–11. http://dx.doi.org/10.1080/15228870902837715.

Tozer, J. (2017, August 6). Trolled again! Outspoken historian Mary Beard in online row over black Roman soldier. *Daily Mail.* https://www.dailymail.co.uk/news/article-4766466/Mary-Beard-online-row-black-Roman-soldier.html.

Traister, R. (2017, May 29). Hillary Clinton is furious. And resigned. And funny. And worried. *New York Magazine.* https://nymag.com/intelligencer/2017/05/hillary-clinton-life-after-election.html.

Traister, R. (2018, September 29). Fury is a political weapon. And women need to wield it. *The New York Times.* https://www.nytimes.com/2018/09/29/opinion/sunday/fury-is-a-political-weapon-and-women-need-to-wield-it.html.

Tronick, E. Z. (1989). Emotions and emotional communication in infants. *American Psychologist, 44*(2), 112–119. http://dx.doi.org/10.1037/0003-066X.44.2.112.

Turkel, A. R. (2000). The voice of self-respect: Women and anger. *Journal of the American Academy of Psychoanalysis and Dynamic Psychiatry, 28*(3), 527–539. https://doi.org/10.1521/jaap.1.2000.28.3.527.

Turkle, S. (2021). *The empathy diaries: A memoir.* Penguin Press.

Van der Kolk, B. (2014). *The body keeps the score: Brain, mind, and body in the healing of trauma.* Penguin Books.

VanSickle, A. (2023, December 18). Justice O'Connor, the first woman on the Supreme Court, lies in repose. *The New York Times.* https://www.nytimes.com/2023/12/18/us/politics/sandra-day-oconnor-repose.html.

Vivona, J. M. (2003). Embracing figures of speech: The transformative potential of spoken language. *Psychoanalytic Psychology, 20*(1), 52–66. http://dx.doi.org/10.1037/0736-9735.20.1.52.

Vivona, J. M. (2006). From developmental metaphor to developmental model: The shrinking role of language in the talking cure. *Journal of the American Psychoanalytic Association*, *54*(3), 877–901. http://dx.doi.org/10.1177/00030651060540031501.

Vivona, J. M. (2009). Embodied language in neuroscience and psychoanalysis. *Journal of the American Psychoanalytic Association*, *57*(6), 1327–1360. http://dx.doi.org/10.1177/0003065109352903.

Vivona, J. M. (2012). Is there a nonverbal period of development? *Journal of the American Psychoanalytic Association*, *60*(2), 231–265. http://dx.doi.org/10.1177/0003065112438767.

Vivona, J. M. (2013). Psychoanalysis as poetry. *Journal of the American Psychoanalytic Association*, *61*(6), 1109–1137. http://dx.doi.org/10.1177/0003065113513639.

Vivona, J. M. (2014). Speech as the confluence of words, body, and relationship: Discussion of Harris, Kirshner, and Spivak. *Journal of the American Psychoanalytic Association*, *62*(6), 1081–1086. http://dx.doi.org/10.1177/0003065114558922.

West, L. (2017, November 8). Brave enough to be angry. *The New York Times*. https://www.nytimes.com/2017/11/08/opinion/anger-women-weinstein-assault.html.

Wichert, I. (2015, October 28). What does success look like for women today? *The Guardian*. https://www.theguardian.com/women-in-leadership/2015/oct/28/what-does-success-look-like-for-you.

Williams, J. C., & Dempsey, R. (with Slaughter, A.-M.). (2014). *What works for women at work: Four patterns working women need to know*. New York University Press.

Winnicott, D. W. (1965). *The maturational processes and the facilitating environment*. International Universities Press.

Winnicott, D. W. (1969). The use of an object. *International Journal of Psychoanalysis*, *50*, 711–716.

Winnicott, D. W. (1975). *Through paediatrics to psycho-analysis: Collected papers*. Brunner/Mazel.

Wolf, H. (2021). Female leadership: Difficulties and gifts. *Journal of the American Psychoanalytic Association*, *69*(1), 136–156. http://dx.doi.org/10.1177/0003065121995957.

Wrye, H. K. (2006). Deconstructing the unconscious saboteur: Composing a life with ambition and desire. *International Forum on Psychoanalysis*, *15*(2), 70–80. http://dx.doi.org/10.1080/08037060600621753.

Zeisler, A. (2016, September 10). The bitch America needs. *The New York Times*. https://www.nytimes.com/2016/09/11/opinion/campaign-bitch-america-needs.html.

Zuckerman, J. R. (1988). *Fear of success in traditional and non-traditional women—Integrating the intrapsychic and situational approaches*. [Unpublished doctoral dissertation, Adelphi University.]

Zuckerman, J. R. (2014a). Everybody's talking! Response to discussants. *Psychoanalytic Perspectives*, *11*(3), 306–315. http://dx.doi.org/10.1080/1551806X.2014.938956.

Zuckerman, J. R. (2014b). Look who's talking! The ongoing problem of the female voice. *Psychoanalytic Perspectives*, *11*(3), 265–283. http://dx.doi.org/10.1080/1551806X.2014.938952.

Zuckerman, J. R. (2019). Nasty women: Toward a new narrative on female aggression. *Contemporary Psychoanalysis*, *55*(3), 214–251. http://dx.doi.org/10.1080/00107530.2019.1637392.

Zuckerman, J. R. (2022). "Nasty women"—Mobilizing female aggression to potentiate women and silence the patriarchy. In J. Petrucelli, S. Schoen, & N. Snider (Eds.), *Patriarchy and its discontents: Psychoanalytic perspectives* (pp. 263–284). Routledge.

Index

Note: Page numbers followed by "n" denote endnotes.

For Product Safety Concerns and Information please contact our EU
representative GPSR@taylorandfrancis.com
Taylor & Francis Verlag GmbH, Kaufingerstraße 24, 80331 München, Germany

www.ingramcontent.com/pod-product-compliance
Lightning Source LLC
Chambersburg PA
CBHW050656280326
41932CB00015B/2933

9 781032 759043